Blessings In Disguise

by
Dr. Ralph G. Willie

Cork Hill Press
Indianapolis

Cork Hill Press
7520 East 88th Place, Suite 101
Indianapolis, Indiana 46256-1253
1-866-688-BOOK
www.corkhillpress.com

Trade Paperback Edition: 1-59408-253-7

Library of Congress Card Catalog Number: 2003116221

Printed in the United States of America

1 3 5 7 9 10 8 6 4 2

CONTENTS

PREFACE
WHAT'S IT ALL ABOUT RALPHIE?

All of us have our problems. Most of us do not want to hear about someone else's problems. This is probably true because we all have enough of our own.

Acting on the assumption that "misery loves company," this author has tried to provide insight into how problems affect others with whom we are acquainted. In effect, he has tried to provide a learning experience based on true life experiences which, if accepted at face value should help to provide useful information. After all, we mortals are all in somewhat the same boat. We may each have a different set of oars with which to make our way through life, but we still have a very strong tie based on our human natures as well as various relationships.

Not all tragedies in life are someone else's fault. It is human nature to try to blame someone else when something goes wrong. On the other hand, accidents do happen. People are sometimes in the wrong place at the wrong time. Perhaps we are wronged because we decided to take the wrong turn in the road. Individual freedom is still part of the constitution. At the same time, we do have over 1.6 million people in jails across America. Not everyone that should be in jail is in jail. Presently our county is seeking voter approval on a jail bond. Some $12.5 million for a 437 bed facility will be spent. This situation is not uncommon. Most communities across the country are simply out of quarters for prisoners. Despite the nation's rising crime rate, it is this author's opinion that the majority of Americans can best be described as law abiding citizens. Hopefully the parents of today will see to it that none of their offspring will learn lawlessness from them. After all, "The best thing to spend on your children is time." — *Baptist Trumpet.*

INTRODUCTION

Years ago, this writer had a steady and most dependable co-worker in his office. While she maintained an outward sense of happiness and natural good humor, her philosophy of life gave her away. She lived by the somewhat well worn slogan that, "Life is a beach, and then you die".

It matters little who you are, or where you live in this, the greatest country in the world, you still enjoy benefits that are really unmeasured. You, like me, are spoiled. We truly take things for granted that we should not. For example, our life expectancy is almost forty years longer than it was for the average grand-parent in his time. In our days, we shall see thousands who live past the age of one hundred years. Medical advances and better nutrition are more important than genetics in today's world.

Webster defines a mosaic as a surface decoration made by inlaying small pieces of variously colored material to form pictures or patterns. And so it is with life. Everything we come in contact with; everything we do weaves an individual mosdic. This fact alone leads to much that results in an individual's character and personality.

In April 1995, a well-known sports caster passed away at age 77. Howard Cossell frequently recounted his childhood experiences as a small Jewish boy in Brooklyn, New York. He later changed his name from Cohen in order to escape memories that haunted him as a school boy. One thing that seemed to stay with him was a certain fear he developed when the larger, stronger Catholic boys used to harass him and hound him on his way to and from school. Later, when he became a Major in the army, he ran across one of those bullies who was a PFC.

He suffered a flashback, and was afraid he would, even then, be beaten up by this old antagonist. Yes, we all have our stories to tell. Over the years, our lives as well as our characters have become formed and colored by the various mosaics of which we are such an interwoven part. Hopefully those experiences recounted herein will serve to help understand your particular, pattern as you consider the events that have led to the formation of similar mosaics in the lives of others.

FORWARD

Lying at the heart of this story is pure unadulterated greed. In recent months we have seen the end result of this kind of thinking in the Enron story. Only in America is it possible to pull the wool over the eyes of the public as well as those who specialize in running the stock market.

The unfortunate part of this happening is that many Americans are left without any real support. It is quite possible to lose everything when we put our trust in those who claim they know how to invest our money. It is obvious that their actions are not the result of a well thought out plan. The only plan they have is to grab as much of the total pie as they can.

Admitedly 11 Sep 2001 was a turning point. We found out the great American dream is vulnerable. We learned that a large part of the world has neither love nor respect for our institutions. Of course we have brought this thinking upon ourselves because of our actions. We live in the greatest country in the world. We consume more of the gas and electricity than any other people on a per capita basis. We enjoy many things that others can only dream about. No wonder they are jealous, and want to express that feeling in acts of terrorism.

No, a large pile of cash is not the real goal we should pursue. We need to take a close look at the teachings of the Master. Man has not really changed much in 2,000 years. All he has done is to recognize the possibility of gain at the expense of others. This is a far distant thing than, "loving your neighbor as yourself." In addition, we do not understand what it is like to be pure in spirit. We fail to give any real consideration to being pure in heart. Is it any wonder the majority of the world has no respect for our way of life?

For the first time in about 60 years I spread some steer manure on my property yesterday. Having heard about the possibility of Anthrax in manure, I sought out something to cover my mouth and nose. A simple response to an event in recent months. At the Salt Lake Olympics this year we noted there were some six policemen for every athlete. Yes, we have become paranoid in this country. Go to the airport and you will see 80 year old grandmothers having their bags searched. It is obvious the time has come for a change in our thinking. How can we bring it about without a change of heart? The same could be said concerning the Jews and the Arabs in Palestine.

ESSENTIAL NUMBERED ITEMS

The following numbered items were brought to my attention as a result of the accident dated 29 April 1988.

1. It is important to have an up to date will.
2. Spouses should be familiar with their partner's business affairs.
3. Almost everything we do in life affects someone else.
4. Patience is a virtue.
5. It is just as important to learn how to receive as to give.
6. A friend in need is a friend indeed.
7. In time of need, it helps to trust in God as well as your neighbor.
8. How we react in troublesome times is just as important as the act itself.
9. There are some great medical advances available in our generation.
10. The answer to one's prayers is indeed real.
11. Money itself is not really important.
12. Needed support from one's family and friends can be very helpful.
13. Support in the form of calls and cards is also very helpful.
14. A strong family bond makes it possible to shift responsibility to other members in time of need.
15. It is possible to make difficult decisions under duress.
16. A strong church organization provides many useful benefits for the member.
17. We need to remember that the Lord Jesus Christ is aware of even our smallest needs in times of stress.
18. Knowledge of one's adverse condition is transmitted very rapidly among family, friends, and other church members.
19. One must learn how to accept the unknown happenings in life.
20. Keeping a proper perspective in life's events is essential.
21. Legal aid, counselling, and medical advice is available today.
22. Keeping a positive attitude and planning ahead with understanding helps to reach one's goals.
23. While no one wishes to undergo difficult times, it does provide 20/20 hindsight that can help others as well as oneself.
24. Life is filled with unknown challenges, and it takes more than a 72 hour kit to solve some of them.
25. The darkest cloud does have a silver lining somewhere.

Several facets of this story are contained in other chapters. If it appears the reader is left hanging in mid-air as a result, you have my apologies. As life moves along, we are all carried in one way or another. Sometimes the desired course of movement is interrupted by such things as illness, death, disease or accident. When that happens, certain adjustments need to be made. Still, it seems to be a characteristic of most mortals that as long as they are alive, breathing, and able to use at least part of their mental capacity, they have a desire to do something useful.

While my injuries were neither life threatning or totally debilitating, they did take several months to heal. During that time, I was not able to follow the same routine of physical fitness I had done for the previous fifteen years. Still, I remember getting into the swimming pool even before my teeth were unwired. That particular event did not occur until some eight weeks had passed. It had been my experience over the years that the human body needs regular exercise. Some approaches to that end are better than others. For me, swimming has become number one. In fact, the man who coined the word "Aerobics", Dr. Ken Cooper, has come to the same conclusion in recent years.

When immersed in water, the human body weighs only 13% as much as it does on the bathroom scale. Supported in water, joint movements are enhanced. Greater flexibility results. Anyone who learns how to swim and puts forth some real effort in the water will attest that he is able to stand taller and straighter as a result. In short, it can be the ideal exercise if performed properly. No, it will not cause one to become slimmer or to lose weight unless the diet is also given consideration. In the U.S. of A, we have a habit known as overeating. Perhaps it stems from our stressful lifestyle. Still, sufficient rest coupled with a proper diet and needful exercise can do much to overcome the hurtful ravages of daily living.

Almost anyone who is injured in an acccident has some scars. In my own case, there is the numb lower right lip. In addition, some facial plastic surgery would be in order. And then there is the condition of the left eye. It never did return to its normal place in the socket from which it had become misplaced. Of course, a great number of us Americans are afflicted with type II diabetes as we grow older. Fortunately that problem can often be taken care of through proper exercise as well as some light medication in the form of micronaise, and giving, proper consideration to one's diet.

Last October it was my good fortune to participate in the Huntsman Senior World games program in St. George, Utah. This Senior Olympic event is open to both men and women over age fifty. This past year some 2,700 individuals were there from eight different countries and forty states. They participated in some 15 different sports. Along with the competition, some other useful information was given, and some blood testing done. Anyone can keep track of his cholesterol level, his tri-glycerides and blood sugar if so inclined. In addition, there are other tests that can be most useful. In the case of men, they show a tendency towards cancer of the prostate gland. In fact, the incidence of this disease among men is almost the same as breast cancer in women. Fortunately a new test is helpful in providing information in this regard.

With seven golf courses in the St. George, Utah area, it would seem that nearly everyone there is a golfer. We should see some new faces on the professional golf circuit during the next few years from this area. My main reason for going to "the games", was to play tennis, throw horseshoes, and to enter the new event surrounding the basketball free throw competition. Here one is given twelve free throw shots followed by four three point shots. All together, this would total some 24 points if executed perfectly. I remember watching a former center from Utah State University compete in my age group. He did win the gold medal, but it was somewhat surprising for me to receive the bronze.

The happiest, most friendly group of performers in the games were those who threw horseshoes. I really don't believe former President Bush had anything to do with this event. At least he was not there. In this event, men under 70 years of age throw from 40 feet. Women creep up to 30 feet away from the pit. Those who practice regularly are able to make a "ringer" with nearly every other throw. For novices such as myself, it was necessary to throw 100 shoes in order to determine my percentage of ringers. That figure was used somewhat like the handicap figure in golf to determine winners in each category. It had to be strictly beginner's luck for me to walk away with a silver medal.

We won't say too much about tennis except that it took a full week of action on some 19 courts to play all the matches. Tennis is a popular sport today. While I did make the final 16 in my age group, that was as far as it went. Next year I shall probably swim and watch my wife play tennis.

Only the victims of an accident are in a position to fully understand why there is no communication between themselves and others. When one is recovering from a short term memory loss, it can appear to others that he is pretty well normal in his responses. In other words, he is able to regurgitate nearly everything that has happened in the past - except the immediate happenings.

In this writer's case, he was totally responsive to feel. When that sharp wheel was run over his foot, his leg would immediately jerk. When he was asked who the president of the United States is, he could also supply that information. At the same time, he was unsure of his location, and why he was there.

During those days of forgetfulness, someone else had to make the daily decisions. Someone had to pay the phone bill as well as the mortgage. Not even thinking about these daily facts of living did provide a certain relief. Still, it is somewhat like the drunk who finds that the mortgage is still due even though he was not concerned.

In today's world, having an attorney nearby is essential. This is particularly true when one is required to deal with a huge insurance claim. Insurance companies seem to be quite able to defend themselves at any cost. It is somewhat like dealing with the IRS. As the wheels of justice turn very slowly, there is ample time to review all the facts of the matter. When the attorney for the insurance company came to town, he made a visit with everyone concerned. His job was to find facts which would help to alleviate the cost of settlement.

After going over the details of the event with the victim, the attorney looked at some of the photos that were taken shortly after the accident and was no doubt impressed by the damage to the victim that was most evident. Of course he could have also been impressed by some tears that were provided by the victim in recounting the event itself. At any rate, he did make an interesting statement. He said, "These pictures should be submitted to our office along with my report. They will do more than anything written to substantiate the actual damage which occurred."

As the victim was insured by Blue Cross, they also showed an interest in the event. After all, they did need to come up with some cash in order to have the patient released from the hospital. As a result, they also provided a document for him to sign. In effect this signing provided that Blue Cross would be reimbursed from any funds that would be later received from any insurance settlement. Of course, the attorney's office concerned also had the victim sign a form which provided that they could deduct their fees from any settlement prior to settlement of the account itself.

In retrospect, this accident should have gone to trial. Naturally there would be sizeable costs in doing so. As a result, the attorneys concerned preferred to work towards an out of court settlement. It was felt that the single biggest drawback to a trial was the appearance of the victim. Comparing his appearance today with the photographs taken shortly after the accident could make the matter more difficult. After all, there remained but very few scars or other deformities to point to. After waiting over two years, an offer was submitted for settlement. While the sum was not large, it did permit the insurance company (Blue Cross), the attorneys concerned, and the victim himself an opportunity to all share equally in the pie.

During the first year after the accident, some rather serious decisions had to be made. Among those needing immediate attention were the sale of the dental practice, how to deal with a partnership that went bankrupt, funding for a new business venture, continual legal involvement with two other businesses, and also some useful plans for the future. Several of these events have been addressed elsewhere. Here again, with the advantage of 20/20 hindsight, some of these things would have been dealt with in an entirely different manner.

Within one year ofter the accident, an opportunity was presented which was hard to turn down. Because of experience in multi-family housing, it was felt that this would be the preferred form of business if possible. Such decisions require sizeable sums of money. This can be especially true when dealing with a governmental agency such as the Resolution Trust Corporation. Their properties were offered at a sensible price, but it was necessary to make a bid along with others. In this connection, it was well known that "money spoke with a stronger voice." In other words, although the RTC would underwrite some ventures with a 75% mortgage, they did prefer to get their money out of the project. At the same time, they also required a sizeable sum of up-front cash to proceed with the sale.

The writer's offer was accepted. A deposit of $50,000 was required. After that, financing for a mortgage needed to be found. An agreement was made with a California source. They too wanted $15,000 in an up-front fee. In the final analysis, they fell through, and some $100,000 was lost after making every effort to close the sale. But that is another story as well as another legal matter to be resolved.

Patience is the quality that is needed most just as it is exhausted. Anon.

During classes at school some thirty years ago, the main topic was one that pertained to social behavior. It was important to learn how to classify people as to type. Either they were introverts, ambiverts, or extroverts. These definitions were based on observations of various behavior patterns. Somehow we have gotten away from such things today. We still make some observations pertaining to type of personality. The type A person is a self starter. He plans ahead, then works his plan. Type B individuals are supposed to cultivate fewer ulcers. They live and let live. Their plans and goals are nebulous. In fact they do not exist. As a result, these individuals "roll with the punches". They take life as it comes, one day at a time. They seldom worry and have few migrain headaches.

When Barbara Mandrell was seriously injured in an auto accident early in the 1980's , it did put her in a difficult situation. She was probably number one in the country music field. Her schedule was tight. She was in demand. Yet, she had to stay in bed. Her major injury was a broken leg which made it difficult to move about on stage. She indicated that she was capable of a performance, but refused to do so because she could not give it her best. She was a perfectionist.

Her story about the accident itself is interesting. Interesting because it has been heard before from others who have suffered a similar result. Her last recollection prior to the accident was that she and others had just fastened their seat belts. She has no recollection of hitting another car head on. While the driver of the other car was killed, no one in the Mandrell car was seriously injured except Barbara. Some 14 days later she remembered what it was she had remembered first. It was a discussion with the Doctor concerning what medication she should take. Prior to that, she did answer questions when asked, but does not remember anything about her location or what those questions were. In other words, while she did not suffer an out of body experience, she was mentally unconscious. This story has been repeated elsewhere in this work, and is something that seems to be common with individuals who have had a severe concussion.

Since her recovery, Barbara has gone back on stage. She also performs at county fairs where I saw her about 1985. Bern Williams sums up her personality type when he said, "Indolence said he was too tired. Alibi said he was hurt. Liar said he was busy. Dependability said, "Give me the darn thing, I'll do it."

LOOKING BACK

When one reaches a certain age in life, he may tend to agree with the Swiss writer Henri Amiel who propounds, "To know how to grow old is the master-work of wisdom, and one of the most difficult chapters in the great art of living".

One thing that helps to grow old is to remember friends and associates over the years who have given us something worthwhile as we rubbed shoulders with them. Along the way, we have met others with whom we were not happy to associate. Their acts are more easily forgotten.

Among the former associates was one Dr. Harold Grupe. How well I remember sitting in the evening, in his front room in Portland, Oregon. It was almost like returning home. While his dear wife Lois would prepare something delictible to eat, we would start the digestive juices flowing with a can of peanuts. Somehow that has become a habit over the years. Another habit Harold taught was photography. It was he who helped me as a young dental officer in West Germany to set up my intra-oral camera outfit. The body of that original Exa camera is somewhere among the things that still lie in a box in our garage.

Harold and Lois were popular with the dental officers in the 464th dental detachment for several reasons. First of all, they were happy people. They were guilty of having a pleasant smile on their faces whenever they met someone. In addition, they always had something worthwhile to present. One evening after work, Beverly and I drove some 60 miles northeast on the freeway to Frankfurt. Sitting in the back seat of our 1957 Dodge sedan were Harold and Lois. Our purpose in making that trip was to find the source of real frankfurters. It happened to be found in a certain cafe known to the Grupes. Soon we also learned what it was like to ingest the real McCoy along with a Liberal amount of horseradish. Yes, those were days to remember. On another occasion, we went to Mannheim and listened to a young man from Texas who had recently won an award in Russia for playing the piano. Van Cliburn was his name.

The only unfortunate part of this story was that we lost Dr. Grupe much too soon. On one occasion he made a trip to Alaska to teach the dentists there about Periodontology. Being unable to resist taking a fishing trip out into the bay, the boat they used hit a rock or some other obstruction, and the passengers ended up in some cold water. Unfortunately Harold was not among the living when rescue was made.

WHERE DOES CONSCIENCE ENTER IN?

Christians have lived for generations with some strange beliefs. Take the Apostles creed for example. Speaking about the Lord Jesus, it says - "He descended into heaven, sittith at the right hand of God; from thence he shall come to judge the living and the dead." More could be cited, but in short, this belief in the Godhead leaves much to be desired.

Because of apostasy from the pristine church, it became necessary in the fourth century to set certain creeds of belief. After all, there was no more revelation, and the scriptures were filled. At the same time, these same creeds were modified from time to time to suit those in authority at the time. For the most part, they have served more than the scriptures themselves as the modified doctrine of the church.

Every person born into this world is endowed with the Light of Christ to serve as his or her conscience. Of course all of us have our free agency to either accept this source of knowledge or to ignore it. Unless we really study theology, and come to know what is right and true by virtue of the Holy Ghost, we never really come to the full use of what we might call, "our conscience".

It is obvious in today's world that most of humanity have chosen to forget the real use of their conscience. Otherwise we would be able to witness a sense of moral goodness or blameworthiness of one's conduct, intentions and character as exhibited in right living, honesty, and truthfulness in every day conduct. Since that is most often absent, we must conclude such individuals have never tried very hard to "fine tune" that which they were given in the beginning.

In the beginning, every man's conscience is clean and pure. It only becomes blackened through sin in later life. We are told age 8 is the age of accountability. That is therefore, the age at which the child is to be baptized and told to "Receive the Holy Ghost". Without that gift it is impossible to really gain a testimony of Jesus Christ. One may arrive at another conclusion, but it is only through knowledge given by inspiration that the truth can be known. It is well for all of us to try our best not to let our conscience become burdened with remorse because of wrong doing. The free exercise of conscience is one of those inalienable rights of man, and is to be guaranteed by governmental laws and even the constitution itself. Of course it is up to us to make the most of this freedom.

CRUNCH TIME

As we go through life, we can all point to times when we had our backs against the wall. In other words, we were between a rock and a hard place. Those who have run a marathon know what this means for the human body. After the first twenty miles, they "hit the wall" as they say. The human body has its limitations. As we tend to age, we become more susceptible to type II diabetes, low thyroid and high cholesterol. All of these conditions need to be addressed with proper medication in order to avoid more serious conditions later on.

We received an interesting telephone call yesterday. It was our eldest son calling from another state. After mentioning the weather, what we wanted to hear was told. His wife Melissa had given birth to their second child. About seven in the morning, she was having contractions about every seven minutes. The physician in charge was called. He suggested they come in within the next thirty minutes. Apparently there was no hurry to do so. The child was born about 9:55 a.m. It was a normal healthy boy some 8 Ibs. 2 ozs. in weight, and 20 inches long. This birth was relatively easy compared to their first child, and it was good to know this crunch time was treated so casually.

Recently we saw some 168 people killed in an Oklahoma City blast. This was a real tragedy in our country. It had never happened before. Last week, an earthquake in Russia killed about 2,500 people. Since this event was far from home, we did not see much of it on T.V. In fact, most of the victims lay under rubble from the apartments in which they lived. Locally we read more about a hurricane in Mass., that killed three people. Crunch time varies from place to place. It would seem that it all depends upon WHO is affected.

It happens nearly every year in the NBA playoffs. With 15 seconds left on the clock, Orlando came down the floor and scored a three point shot. Mr. Miller of Indiana was not to be outdone. His three point shot took place with 5.3 seconds left to play. However, the game was far from over. Tom Hardaway scored for Orlando with 1.3 seconds left, giving Orlando a one point lead. After a couple of time outs, Indiana threw the ball in to their seven foot center. Rick Smits who faked out a player just above the foul line. His shot was in the air when the buzzer sounded. The final score was 94 to 93 for Indiana

Life is seldom as dramatic as many things that happen on the T.V. programs. One of my favorite shows is the Rockford Files. In trying to determine why that is, I have concluded that it seems to center around a certain sense of humor which is not always associated with a tragic happening. On one occasion Mr.

Rockford was treated to a lunch provided by an active model. After the second serving of wheat thins, he promptly indicated that he was now ready to go out and stop a freight train.

Of course the ultimate in crunch time is associated with matters of life and death. Perhaps that is why I went into Dentistry instead of Medicine. At any rate few of us look forward to the time when we personally must come to grips with life in the next sphere. Perhaps our greatest concern revolves around the fact that we have very little knowledge with which to meet the great beyond. The unknown is always more frightening. Of course the finality of death is something with which we desire not to come to grips with, even though we may have faith in life after death.

It was just over one year ago now when my younger brother received a phone call from a nurse in a Senior Citizen's center. Apparently our father's blood pressure had dropped precipetiously. My brother immediately went to our father's room and noted that Dad was resting easily. While observing the patient in bed for a few minutes, he heard a deep sigh associated with a final deep breath. Our father was gone. This was his "crunch time". Not too many of us will get out of this life any other way.

CHAPTER I

There's a destiny that makes us brothers.
None goes his way alone. All that we send
into the lives of others, will come back into
our own. — Edwin Markham

As she approached the sliding door that led to the deck outside the house, Leisa was filled with fear and trepidation. After all, the most important man in her young life was waiting there. Over twenty years had gone by, and now it comes down to a certain difficult meeting. In this case it was not casual. This particular time and place had come as the result of two weeks of continuous concern. During that time Leisa had spent countless hours in telephone conversations with friends and relatives. It had been her reports that fortified others and provided information which helped to allay concern.

As life goes along its unpredictible course, each of us is beset with challenges and fears of various kinds. Just how these difficulties are met and disposed of varies from person to person. Some things are dispensed with in a simple stroke of the pen. Others seem to last for an eternity. As a result, the after effects can be excruciating. Fortunately, the passage of time serves as an effective healer. In her own words, Leisa described the afore mentioned meeting in the following terms: "It was a sunny day, or at least a clear day because it wasn't raining. Mom and Dad were sitting out on the deck. Dad was facing out, with the back of his head towards the living room. I did not know what to do or what to expect. I've always been Daddy's little girl, and it was hard for me to open the glass door. My Dad was sitting there in the chair, but it was so hard to know he had been through all that had happened. For some reason Dad was supposed to always be here. I was told that if Dad was going to live he would end up with poor eyesight, brain damage or something very serious.

"I walked slowly out onto the deck. My Dad turned around, and he looked so sore. His eyes were pools of blood. He just tried to smile, reached out his arms and acted like everything was O.K. and everything was going to work out all right. He was surely a strength to all of us. If it were me, I probably would not even wanted to see my own family. Of course Dad has his pride, and he did not want to get out and mingle with others immediately. Still, when his head returned to normal, and we told the story to many others, people were understanding and helped us all a lot."

PLEASE DEAR GOD, MAKE MY WORDS TODAY SWEET
AND TENDER, FOR TOMORROW I MAY HAVE TO EAT THEM.

"It was about two o'clock in the morning when the phone call came. I was on duty as a Sgt. in the U.S. Air Force stationed in North Carolina. At the time we were busy loading a cargo plane, and were in the middle of an exercise. When I did get to the telephone to return the call, the news was indeed disturbing. My father had been seriously injured in an auto accident and was even now undergoing surgery in Chico, California.

At the time, only one thing entered my mind. I must try to get to California. But how? By following my best hunch, I immediately incurred the wrath of my commanding officer. Bursting into his office in the presence of other officers brought an immediate response. If you have ever heard a Stevedore swear, you will know what I mean. Fortunately for me, his tune changed completely when he heard the news".

"Hurry on home," said he. "Let me know if there is anything at all that we can do to help".

"My first act was to gain some additional information. Being in the military, I could still be on the payroll if given emergency leave. After all, I did not feel my mother should be at the bedside all alone".

"At the request of my Captain, the Red Cross got me a ticket on Delta Airlines to San Francisco. The plane was due to leave in four hours. Fortunately everything fell into place. After flying all day on Saturday, I was rewarded by a room in the Marriott Airport Hotel at the courtesy of my brother who worked as a hotel manager. Unfortunately there was no local air traffic out to Chico until the next morning. Meanwhile, I was able to speak to my mother, and found someone at the airport to meet me upon my arrival on Sunday morning. It was not long until I slipped into a chair next to mother at the Church services".

"My mother and two of the nurses on duty tried to prepare me for what I was going to see in the intensive care unit at the Chico hospital. The patient, my father, was heavily bandaged. His arms were tied down to the bed. There were tubes from both mouth and nose, and wires seemed to run in every direction. The patient reminded me of a Halloween Jack o'Lantern that had been left out in the rain. In other words, he looked both swollen and soggy".

"Over the years, my duties in the Air Force have taken me to such far away places as Germany and Panama. Some of our missions involved the removal of the dead. In other instances, I have also seen people die in accidents. Somehow my visit to the hospital this time affected me differently. This event was much more personal, and affected someone who had been close to me for over twenty years. As a result, my emotions were very much on the surface. It helped quite a lot when my father extended his hand to me and clasped it tightly.

Upon leaving the intensive care unit, some of my pent up feelings emerged. How, I wondered, could something like this happen? In the other room lay a man who had never purposely injured anyone else. My fists automatically clenched and I wondered who was to blame? What could be done?

It became clear to me later, the truck driver who was on the wrong side of the road was indeed culpable. In America, such people are sued. Interestingly enough, this truck driver placed a call to the hospital. In speaking with him, it was obvious he was indeed sorry for what had happened. He apologized profusely. This had been his first serious accident in 38 years of driving. He expressed genuine concern for the victim and indicated his insurance coverage would be adequate to defray all costs involved. My adverse feelings towards this man were mollified".

"As occurs in most accidents, legal advice is usually required. It was our good fortune to have a local attorney introduced to us who had experience in matters of this nature. He came to the hospital and gave us some advice. Together we returned to the scene of the accident . We met with the officer in charge, and received information concerning potential witnesses. We went to the local paper and found the accident had been given local coverage. We even searched the crumpled automobile to see if we could find my father's two front teeth. This search was not successful.

In hindsight, we noted that it took two years for the legal matters to be resolved. There was no million dollar settlement. In fact, after the hospital bills and the attorney were paid, it soon became obvious who the real winners were".

CHAPTER II

WHEN SHOULD ONE QUIT?

The true story is told of one Lawrence Hanratty. No, one cannot ascribe his problems to his name. Lawrence indicates he has died three different times, and is now considered to be a modern day miracle. A carpenter by trade, Lawrence was nearly electrocuted in 1984 while simply doing his job. Since then, things have not improved. As a result of this event, Lawrence was in a coma for several weeks which left him permanently disabled. In an attempt to recover medical benefits as well as to regain his former job, he hired four different law firms. His first attorney was disbarred. The next two counselors died with their boots on. Another law firm lost his file, another wanted a mere $3,000 as an up-front fee.

Many of us can point to lawyers who have simply failed to do their duty. Lawrence can also point to one who ran off with his wife as well. Because of the accident, Lawrence has been hooked up to a tank of oxygen continuously, and has been taking some 42 pills every day. In 1989 he also lapsed back into a coma for several weeks. He suffers from depression, heart trouble, a bad liver, and has agoraphobia. The latter will prevent him from working in open spaces.

Mr. Hanratty is only 38 years of age. Just six months ago, someone stole his car and totalled it. After the police left, a kid came along with a gun and robbed him of $250. As if that was not enough, his insurance company now wishes to cut off his benefits, and his landlord is trying to boot him out of his apartment. Fortunately a local psychiatrist is willing to treat him without charge.

Lawrence Hanratty has been denied medicaid, Social Security and welfare. He has been surviving on a workmen's compensation check in the amount of $540 per month. Since another doctor testified that Lawrence was capable of returning to work, he has lost his workman's compensation. Last month, his insurance company cut him off without any benefits.

Fortunately some fellow workers and a local tenants group have been lobbying for him, and have found a friendly grocer to provide food. The most important thing in his favor is his attitude.

"There's always hope," says Hanratty. "When you start to give up ....you can pack it in".

HELP THY BROTHER'S BOAT ACROSS, AND LO! THINE OWN HAS REACHED THE SHORE — Hindu Proverb

Many people have learned over the years that they can only count on certain individuals to respond when the chips are down. In other words, a friend in need is a friend indeed. Although there may be times when cold hard cash is involved, this particular treatise applies only to other forms of assistance. As we all know, help may be needed in several different ways at several different times.

With reference to the accident mentioned else where, two people were primarily involved. Both had been sitting in the back seat of the sedan when it was side swiped by the truck and trailer. One of these was shipped to another city by helicopter while the other was released from the hospital and went in another direction to catch an airplane home to Seattle.

Where the assistance entered in was when the released person stopped at a local motel and picked up the belongings, camera and billfold of the one shipped to another hospital by helicopter and returned them to this person's home intact. That was something the other person was unable to do for himself.

It is interesting to see how some people perform under rather adverse circumstances. We have all heard the story of the person who lifted an automobile off the body of a victim. Sometimes that person then becomes a victim as well. Psychological injury is just as real as physical injury. Such seemed to happen here. The person who flew home became dependent upon sleeping pills and other medical help in order to cope with the effects of the accident to the other person.

In many traumatic incidents, the victim is oftimes deprived of actual knowledge of the event itself. This can be a blessing in disguise. After all, if he or she is unaware of the injury, and does not become a victim of aftershock, the chance of recovery is improved. Many lives have been lost when the victim is unable to cope with the symptoms as well as the looks of the injury itself. In this particular instance, the victim was unable to recount the events surrounding the accident itself, so it becomes necessary to review what happened with the second person in the back seat of the automobile.

"We were on highway S-20 near Grass Valley, CA. Going along an upgrade, I noticed a truck coming towards us. The truck was on our side of the road, I yelled to our driver to get off the highway. He got over into the ditch. The semi-truck coming our way was trying to get back onto his side, but the highway was slippery. All of a sudden, the 48 or 50 foot trailer jack-knifed and started to tip over. It appeared the wheels on the driver's side were about three feet off the ground. I was sure we would all be killed. Everything happened so fast, there was no time to do anything. From what I remember, I went up over the front seat and ended up on the dashboard. The next thing I remembered was that I was on a stretcher.

Looking over to the person who had been next to me, I recognized that it was the Doctor; but what a mess. I hoped he was still alive. The other two men were injured, but released from the hospital the following day. I had severe pains which were X-rayed, but the Doctor said I could be released. I asked about a ride to Reno. One fellow drove me to a bus stop where they came by every hour. I retreived the camera and went to the motel in Reno.

There I contacted the local police to obtain permission to pick up the Doctor's baggage as well as my own.

When I got to the airport, they would not let me on the airplane. Obviously I was walking with a certain reel to my gait. I had to tell them I did not drink. I did not go into the specifics of the accident I had been through, otherwise they may have called an airport physician.

As a veteran, I went to a local hospital two days in a row. The military suggested that I rest and take these pills. Of course my injuries were not all physical. I have not been normal since. My system has never returned to normal. I underwent a three way by-pass and have been on constant medication.

I never, never want to be in another automobile accident like the one we went through. You know I will always do whatever I can for you. I have the feeling we will always be friends".

It was James Howell who said, "Respect a man, he will do the more". Sometimes, and in some things, we cannot do any more.

THE RAREST OF GEMS

TRUE Friendship is as rare as the Hope diamond. It has close relatives in honesty, dependability and trust. Many poems have been written on this theme, and most of them conclude that to have a friend, one must first be a friend.

Human relations seem to contain something of the Divine when they are REAL. These deep, important and lasting ties that bind one person to another are the stuff of which eternities are made.

Without serious friend to friend relationships, life becomes devoid of hope, dreams, a reason to share, and a reason to strive for the best that is in us. I effect, it lacks a thing called SUBSTANCE.

While many of life's problems seem to result from our relationships with others, only once in a great while do we come in contact with someone with whom we can truly empathize. Someone to whom we can relate without saying much. Such occasions are both uncommon as well as unusual.

Someone has said that life's greatest form of communication is not mouth to ear, but rather heart to heart. Such relationships can provide relief from the vicissitudes of life, and lend meaning to why we are here.

SOMEDAY the rarest of gems will appear. Will I be ready to fulfill my part?

THE ACCIDENT

While returning to his office one day about three months after the accident, the Doctor was stopped by a man whom he did not recognize. He turned out to be the husband of a dental assistant that was presently employed in another nearby office. This individual called the Doctor by name, and indicated he had been praying for him daily since the accident occurred. Later information indicated that other friends and patients had been doing the same. Such interest and concern is heartening in the world today. Consider what had happened to Connie, an employee of the Doctor for some sixteen years.

Connie hurried back to Federal Way from Moscow, Idaho where she had been for the weekend. She had been informed that someone had been injured in an accident. Her son, a checker at the local Safeway store, had phoned and left that message with her son in Moscow. Details were sketchy. Upon her return to the Safeway store, Connie immediately found her son. He was busy checking out groceries for a customer. When she was told the victim of the accident had apparently experienced a "crushed head", she broke into tears and ran from the store. No doubt this display of emotion was unusual in the store and several customers wondered what it was all about.

But what about the accident? One could read the policeman's report. There one could learn that it happened on a two lane state highway in the state of California on 29 April 1988 at approximately 2:30 p.m. That same report indicated there were four men in a Chrysler automobile when it was side-swiped by a truck and trailer. The Chrysler had been driven some fifty feet from the point of impact, and ended up against a 10 foot embankment. Had the impact occurred some 50 feet further down the road, the Chrysler would have gone off a steep cliff. The driver of the truck was shocked. He had later reported that this was his first accident in 38 years of driving.

Fortunately not all occupants of the car were seriously injured. Two of them had some minor injuries. The other two were unconscious and needed transportation by ambulance to the Grass Valley hospital. One of them later reported that he had been reading a paper in the back seat of the car, but looked up just in time to see the truck come towards the car. He later awoke just in time to see the other unconscious passenger carried into the hospital. This was a frightening experience for him.

MAN'S GREATEST GIFT - A GOOD WIFE

It was about three o'clock on a Friday afternoon. As I had just returned home from a trip out of state, I was engaged in conversation with one of my best friends over the telephone when our local operator butted in with the request we hang up so an emergency message could be received. On the other end of the line was the Sheriff in Grass Valley, California. He declared that my husband had been seriously injured in a recent auto accident, and although he was alive, it appeared he had a fractured skull and other serious injuries. He was in an ambulance on his way to the local hospital. He further stated that a doctor from the hospital would be calling me soon.

My immediate response was to drop to my knees in prayer. It was not only my husband who needed succor and a healing influence, but it was also obvious to me that I had serious needs myself. Soon the second phone call arrived. The physician at the Grass Valley hospital gave me news which was even more alarming. My husband would be flown by helicopter to Chico, some 90 miles away since they had a trauma team who could provide the services required.

How could I possibly find my way to Chico, CA? I had been near there once when my husband and I flew our private plane to a small community nearby, by the name of Paradise. I was in Seattle, Washington and no longer had a pilot of my own. I knew our friends in Paradise would like to be alerted, so I gave them a call and hoped they could meet the helicopter. Since I also had a friend standing by and wondering what my emergency was, I got back to her as well.

Naturally the best approach to arrive somewhere in a hurry is to go there by plane. My call to the airport disclosed that a plane to Sacramento would be leaving within the hour. It would arrive by way of Reno and Las Vegas. Unfortunately I would be placed on a list as the fifth person on standby.

While my mind was racing wildly, I knew I must get to the airport immediately. What would happen there was in the hands of the Almighty. As I started out my front door, who should arrive but my faithful friend with whom I had been speaking earlier. She had come to stay with me in the event I would need to stay home overnight.

Despite my desires, it was obvious that my chances of flying out of Seattle were doubtful. I could only wait patiently while other names and numbers were called to board the plane. Yes, I had made it to the proper location in time to board the plane. More importantly, four of the five scheduled to fly standby failed to show up. Somehow I was awarded the last seat on the flight to Reno. So far, so good.

Just before the plane landed in Las Vegas, my name was called over the loud speaker. I was to phone home before catching my flight to Sacramento. It was my youngest daughter. She informed me that a neighbor of ours had a friend in Sacramento who would meet me at the airport and drive me the 90 miles north to Chico. What an evening this had been!

Upon my arrival at the hospital in Chico, I was greeted by my two friends who had driven there from Paradise. They had seen my husband as he had been admitted to the hospital. The only comment about that which I can remember is, "He didn't look good at all". It was 2:30 in the morning. Some twelve hours had passed since my husband's accident. At the moment he was lying in the recovery room, his head completely swathed with bandages. Even his eyes were covered. The nurses in charge said he had come through six and one-half hours of surgery. Other than that, their knowledge of his condition was not much better than mine.

Two weeks of waiting, worrying, and wondering in a hospital can be very unnerving. During that period of time, my husband lost twenty pounds. While I cannot say the same, it was a time of serious reflection. In time of need, it is wonderful to have friends. It was at once apparent to me what the Savior meant when he said we should love one another."

—AND NOW FOR THE REST OF THE STORY

Try putting yourself in the shoes of two individuals who participated in this true life drama. As a woman, and wife, you like to shop. Suppose you had spent another hour in the stores. You would not have been home to receive the Sheriff's phone call. His information was necessary in order for you to get to the airport in time to catch the plane that day.

As the daughter, tired from work and shopping, you were mostly asleep when you heard a phone ring in the next room. "Oh, let mother get it", you thought to yourself as slumber took hold. Several minutes later you were suddenly awakened when the noisy sliding door to your room was opened. When you saw your mother's face, you became fully awake. She had the appearance as one who was not really there. She had the look of some far off concern. And it all began.

Later, as you found yourself at the ticket office at the airport, you heard the clerk tell your mother her chances of flying to Las Vegas that evening were really very poor. If she wanted to become the fifth standby, she could. This statement caused you to shed some obvious tears which did gain the attention of the clerk. Upon learning yours was a bonefide emergency, she suggested that you both hurry to the gate where the plane was waiting and get your name on the list of prospective passengers just as soon as possible.

After leaving the airport, you returned home to hear the phone ring. This was the beginning of a very long night of telephone conversations. Your concern about someone to meet your mother in Sacramento was ameliorated when one of your church leaders appeared and announced that he had already arranged for that to happen.

Of course the other party involved in this event was the mother, who was in the air on her way to Reno. Because of her concerns, she preferred things to be quiet so that she could think. Instead, there was a partly drunken wedding party aboard who did their best to keep a party like atmosphere going all the way to Reno. The next thing that caused concern was an announcement over the loudspeaker on the plane saying you should contact the Steward prior to changing planes in Las Vegas. "What on earth could that be about?", you wondered. Fortunately it was good news. Someone had been contacted to meet you upon your arrival in Sacramento. And so it went on that fateful day in April.

Bachelor: A man who believes in the survival of the fleetest.
— Margaret Eastman

As we go through life we meet people of many types. Some of them will do most anything they can to take advantage of their fellowman, and then make themselves scarce. By the same token, there are enough problems in everyday living to take care of, without having to worry about trying to recover lost funds that disappeared into someone else's hands.

On the front page of today's paper, two things stood out. One pertained to the construction of a new local horse race track. In order to finish this 168 acre project, some 17 acres classified as "wetlands" would need to be filled in. Before that can happen, the army corps of engineers has required that a complete environmental impact statement will need to be filled out. This will result in a time delay of at least three years, with no promise of approval.

By now, those who planned the race track have spent some $4 million. Some suggest politics is involved. Whatever is involved, there will need to be a great deal more time and effort spent in order to determine what the local traffic impact will be, and to also determine how filling in the 17 acres will affect waterfowl in this area. Not that the waterfowl cannot be accommodated in some other area, but simpy because we live in a time when environmental decisions must be made for every site to be developed.

Quoted on the front page of the same paper was a statement taken from Dante. "The final circle of hell is reserved for perpetrators of the most heinous sin of all, betrayal". This quotation was applied to the acts of a convicted pedophile who had apparently molested over 100 youth. Some twenty-two of that number was present at the trial to describe the anguish they had suffered later in life as a result.

While these two events portray some of the problems of society in today's world, most of us are in a position to apply similar thinking to the events which we must deal with individually; which events can be described as personal catastrophies. But, more about that later.

I really must go and clean up the kitchen, and hang up some Christmas lights. Bringing up these two problems on a regular basis is not a very uplifting thing to do from my wife's point of view. As a result, we shall become domestically minded for awhile.

"One of the Greatest Discoveries in Life Is Finding a Dependable Person"
— R. L. Evans

Like most businessmen who rely on others to do most of the work in the office, it took me about 14 years of Dental Practice to find an individual who really lived up to the above description. It is always difficult when interviewing someone to determine whether or not he or she possesses those qualities which the job requires. In this particular instance I was impressed by one who applied, because while worried and somewhat concerned, she was still able to maintain a sense of humor.

It was Winston Churchill who remarked , "In my belief, you cannot deal with the most serious things in the world unless you also understand the most amusing". There are few places in our society where humor is needed more than in a dental office. My brother-in-law used to suggest that there is at least one other place where he would wish to go even less. That place of course, a mortuary.

The person mentioned above was hired, and thereafter found to be the ideal employee. Why? Because many people enjoyed coming to the office simply to have a conversation with her. Someone with an outgoing personality, coupled with the ability to empathize with others is an unusual person indeed. Hanging on her wall was a clipping taken from a dental magazine. It showed a patient playing a violin. Underneath were the words, "Does this mean you are planning not to pay?" Can you imagine being able to extract money from someone while they have a smile on their face at the same time? Such was her talent. Over the years I noted that our collections usually exceeded the amount we put on the books each year.

One will have to admit that if two people can work together for nearly 18 years without serious argument, that record is better than most marriages in today's world. In this regard, one could well speculate why some working relationships work. Perhaps a true to life story will help to illustrate the point.

About thirty years ago a young woman was hired as a new dental assistant by Dr. Richard F. Latemer. At the time, it was intended that the assistant would work for only one year to help set up his practice. Thirty one years later this same assistnat is still working for him. NO, they did not marry, but maintained both separate and distinct lifestyles.

One thing the average worker thinks to be most important, is money. Such workers find that time hangs heavy on their hands, and their life revolves around weekends. A number of surveys have been made to determine what is really most important to an employee. Actual dollar income was not high on the list. In fact, it usually came in fourth or fifth. In the case of the assistant mentioned earlier, CONSIDERATION was most important. "Dr. Latemer is very easy to work for, but if I had to stress one thing, it would be his consideration of my other obligations", said she.

Another word that appears high on the list is respect. That thing, coupled with understanding, and a willingness to give, seem to be among the most important values wanted by the employed. In addition, there is one other trait that is especially important. That trait is gratitude. An expression of appreciation for another person's efficiency and adaptability is always in order.

As Dr. Latemer said, "She has assumed responsibilities, but has never tried to take over, or to run the show. Her cheerful attitude has made working with her a pleasure for over thirty years".

The significance of this information should be stressed. We often hear much about "stressful occupations". Air traffic controllers have been mentioned as working under difficult conditions. Other professions have been included, such as surgeons, airplane pilots, Presidents, and others who make serious decisions in their work. If one consults the statistics regarding professions and their number of sucides, rated at the top of the list are dentists. The reasons for this are many and varied. One can only speculate as to the main reason. One thing is for sure, early in his career, a dentist must learn how to cope with people in his pratice who would rather not be there. Being told daily that you are not liked can get to you. In my class of 75, I can think of at least three who decided to make a permanent solution to a temporary problem by taking the suicide approach. In all instances, it created more problems for someone else than it helped.

There is an old Bulgarian proverb that states, "Your own calamity is more useful to you than another's triumph". After all, we all learn best from experience. At the same time, there are few things that are sought after more than simple recognition for a job well done. Some time ago I had a high level meeting with an employee of the Internal Revenue Service. After going over the facts and figures we came to a mutual conclusion. While not completely happy with the result, I wrote the person a letter of appreciation for her willingness to review the facts of the matter. She replied that this was the first letter of appreciation she had ever received in some 25 years of service.

Recently a lab technician of mine gave me a call. I had written him a letter explaining in detail just how good his workmanship had been on a certain case. In his conversation he indicated the part he liked best was where I mentioned how nice the bridgework looked when seated in the patient's mouth. That is one phase of his work he could never see or appreciate. After making final payment on some furniture I had purchased, I received a letter that expressed thanks for my payment, and an expression of appreciation to me as a customer. That same approach was used in my dental practice with good results. Several people let me know this was the first time they had ever received such recognition from any business with which they had done business in the past. I have often wondered to what extent this simple expression of thanks influenced their future behavior when it came time to "pay the bill".

On television we often see a close up of some athlete who simply says, "Hi Mom!" Mothers should be given more praise and appreciation. One thing I learned early in life was a concept that has been most useful over the years. That concept is best expressed in these words, "If you can't say something nice about another person, it is best not to say anything at all". In keeping with this same concept, it is also sensible to employ the use of positive expressions when dealing with our fellow human beings. No one is perfect, and the ability to accept people as they are is another key to getting along in the workplace. It has been my observation that those who get along best are those who do not criticize others either openly or behind their backs, but who are willing to live and let live.

In keeping with the theme of this work, I should like now to provide information relating to the thoughts and actions of the person who worked with me for nearly 18 years after she was advised of the aforementioned accident. This will come principally from recorded words of this person herself.

Ralph G. Willie

The Deepest Urge in Human Nature is the Desire to be Important
—John Dewey

Some eleven years had gone by since Connie had been employed outside the home on a regular basis. She now felt ready to return to the job market. As a result, she answered an ad in the local paper, and made an appointment for an interview. That interview was favorable, and it appeared she was back to work in a dental office.

After the first day of work, some doubt arose. It was very annoying to realize just how many things had changed over the years. The multiplicity of insurance forms was mind boggeling. After all, a tooth was still a tooth, but the increased pile of papers required an unusual effort. Her initial response was, "I'm not really sure whether I can do this work".

Things did not seem to improve much during the next two weeks. Somehow the demands of the front office increased. Connie had decided to quit. She explained her situation to the Doctor in charge. He suggested that an understanding be made. If she did not feel competent after six months on the job, they would then part company with no regrets. After all, the time could someday come when she might need to work for a living. What would happen to her self-confidence if she were to quit now? The suggestion was accepted. At the end of six months, Connie simply loved the job. She knew she had found her niche. Besides, if she planned to stay on the job, it was time to buy a second uniform. And so she did!

Connie and her husband Dan had gone to Moscow, Idaho for the weekend. Her second son Greg, was playing football for the University of Idaho. While there, one of the son's roommates told Connie someone had been trying to reach her by telephone. It was her first son, Mike. She returned the call, and found the news to be disturbing. She learned the Doctor concerned had been in an auto accident in California and he had suffered a fractured skull. He was now in surgery. About all she or anyone else could do, was to wait.

Upon her return home, Connie immediately went to the Safeway store where Mike was working as a checker. All she was able to learn was that things did not look good. As she broke into tears and started to leave the store, the customers in line had to wait while Mike ran after her to offer comfort.

Another Dentist in the clinic had tried to reach Connie at this time. As he was in another part of the building, he was unsure of her last name. After a few calls he found someone who knew, and received her home telephone number. He encouraged Connie to come in and talk to him the following Monday.

"Golly, things were quiet in the office. In fact, it was sort of spooky", said Connie. "As a result, I took the books home where I could call and re-appoint patients without feeling like I was in some sort of mortuary". After the conversation with the neighboring doctor on Monday, she felt better. While it appeared things with the accident victim were "touch and go", it helped to talk about it. In fact, Connie was encouraged by one of the patients in the practice to call the hospital and gain some first hand information. This approach helped both her and the Doctor's wife, who was at his bedside.

It soon became obvious the accident in question was no "fender bender". In fact, it was not possible to re-appoint patients for an indefinate time. Another difficulty was in trying to explain the patient's condition to the numerous curious people who called. What does one say? Naturally it is good to be optomistic, but without any real evidence to that effect, explanations become limited. One helpful thing that occurred was the heartfelt thoughts and suggestions received from numerous friends and patients who had become very close over the years. The thoughts and concerns of others was indeed helpful to all concerned.

After the Doctor had been home for a week or two, it became obvious he would not be doing any more dental work soon. The practice would need to be sold. Meanwhile, it was important to collect as many outstanding accounts as possible, and to take care of those who were in need of dental care. These things were accomplished.

Within three months the practice was sold. Connie elected to stay with the new owner. In fact, she became the most important asset. Human beings are creatures of habit. If they feel comfortable some place, they will return. Connie made them feel comfortable. Although Connie does not like change, she felt good about the new owner even though it required knowledge of the computer as well as longer hours on the job. After a year or two, it became obvious that it was time for another change. Not all personalities blend without friction. Even though a Chinese proverb indicates that a gem cannot be polished without friction; friction still takes its toll.

CHAPTER III

AN ACCIDENTAL INTRODUCTION

Arnt Dybvik had three brushes with death in a single day. The lucky dentist of Nordland County, Norway, first crashed his car into another on an icy hill. While he checked the damage, a third auto slammed into Dybivk's car, which rolled into the dentist and broke his arm. Dybvik then jumped into a taxi to go to the hospital, but on the way the cab was demolished in a three car crash.

"I'm just glad it didn't get any worse", Dybvik said later as he recovered from his injuries.

There are a number of conclusions that one can make from reviewing accidental injury. He or she could say, "Shucks, I just happened to be in the wrong place at the wrong time". Others might feel there was a certain God granted interest in their time of trouble. Still, others who may be superstitious would claim, "It all came because of something I should have been able to avoid".

Whatever the actual reason. Bill Murray counsels that we should "Live every day to its fullest, because you never know how many more of them you're going to get". This would leave one to believe that an old quotation by Vauvenargues would not be worth reviewing. "There are those who are so scrupulously afraid of doing wrong they seldom venture to do anything". Another thought is presented by George Eliot when he says, "Our deeds act upon us as much as we act upon them". And then there is an old Yiddish proverb that suggests, "A man should live if only to satisfy his curiosity".

Yes, life is filled with philosophies of different kinds. If one can find something that leads to a certain peace of mind as he goes along life's many corridors, so much the better. Recently we read about a certain shooting at the local mall which led to the death of a sixteen year old person. This represents a sad and unfortunate symptom of society today. Violence has become commonplace. Soon the citizens of the good old USA will all be armed to the teeth with a weapon of some kind. Perhaps we have all been watching too many western movies. Unfortunately this is not a major cause of the problem.

In conclusion, a thought from the pen of Richard C. Miller may prove to be of value. "The best way to find peace of mind is to stop looking for it".

Much of the above information is similar to that reported in the *Grass Valley News* on 30 April 1988. "A Seattle, Washington man was critically injured and three others taken to Sierra Nevada Memorial Hospital following a Friday afternoon accident on Highway 20, three miles north of Nevada City. Details were not immediately available, but preliminary reports indicate a car and semi-trailer truck were involved. Here, the Seattle accident victim later reported he did not recall the accident. In fact, when he looked in a mirror some 13 days later, he simply asked, "What happened? Where am I?"

In the case of the sky diver, Jill Shields 31, said at the metro Health Medical Center, "I am the luckiest person you've ever seen". Witnesses who were sky diving at the same time reported that Jill had fallen some 10,500 feet and landed in a swamp filled with mud. She did suffer spinal bone fractures, a fracture of a small bone in the pelvis area, at least two broken ribs, and many bruises. Still she declared, "Whatever I'm supposed to be doing, I haven't done yet".

Bobby Hurley mentioned earlier is still recuperating. It is felt he should still be able to play professional basketball, assuming his lungs respond to treatment. One of them was partially detached in the accident. The police report in his case says, "Hurley, driving home in his small pick-up truck made a left turn, and was struck on the driver's side by a 1970 Buick station wagon driven by Dan Wieland, a 37 year old Sacramento resident. Wieland, who suffered a fractured right leg, was traveling about 55 mph without headlights at the time of the accident. Neither Wieland nor Hurley was believed to be under the influence of alcohol or drugs", police said.

May I simply conclude this accident report with a final quotation concerning Bobby Hurley, "It was so hard to see him that way. I didn't realize how serious it was. He's such a physically strong person, and then to see him in this condition, words just can't describe it". Such comments are common to all similar accidents it seems. Not only is one person a victim, but the effects of an accident influence others in many ways as well.

Highway 20 accident — A Seattle, Wash., man was critically injured and three others taken to Sierra Nevada Memorial Hospital following a Friday afternoon accident on Highway 20, three miles north of Nevada City. Details were not immediately available, but preliminary reports indicate a car and semi-trailer truck were involved. The Washington state resident, identified by officials at N.T. Enloe Memorial Hospital in Chico as Ralph Willie, 60, was listed this morning in critical condition. He was flown there from SNMH by helicopter. One of the other three, identified by SNMH officials as Charles Nelson, was admitted; he was listed in satisfactory condition this morning. The other two, August Kreiger and Lee Franklin, were treated and released. No ages or hometowns for the SNMH patients was immediately available. The California Highway Patrol is investigating.

Why is it that many accidents seem to be tragically similar? In one of my files is a sheet of paper entitled, "Saved by the Belt Award". This is to certify that a Doctor Blank was saved on 29 April 1988, from serious injury or death because of his use of an automotive safety system; and is hereby recognized as a "SAVED-BY-THE-BELT" survivor of Washinton State. The above recognition is signed by the governor of the state.

To an extent, this sort of information is meant to be publicized so that others may recognize the need to always wear a seat belt when traveling in an automobile. At times such information is used on television or in the paper. Still, we see far too many deaths from automobile accidents in this country every year. Of course, accidental death is only one way to die. It was recently reported that AIDS had claimed some 170,000 American lives by the end of 1992. This is nearly three times the number of U.S. soldiers that were lost in the war in Vietnam. In 1993, it is predicted some 7,500 American children will have contracted AIDS before birth or from breast feeding after birth. Perhaps auto accidents are not quite so serious after all.

Yes, seat belts do have a use while traveling in an automobile. In my case, my insurance company paid me some $15,000 simply because I was wearing a seatbelt. A certain professional basketball player was not so fortunate when he had an accident recently. May I quote from the report as given in the local paper (*Sacremento Bee*, December 19, 1993). "Bobby Hurley's Toyota 4-runner was sent 125 feet from the point of impact. Hurley, who wasn't wearing a seat belt, was ejected and landed in a drainage ditch". As a result, it was said of Mr. Hurley, "He can't talk, and his eyes are swollen shut. But he was nodding and shaking his head when we were saying things to him", one person reported.

"We didn't ask him about the accident, so I don't know if he knows what happened to him", said one reporter. "His parents were trying to put on a brave face with him, but you know how they must have felt inside when they saw him". "We are all just thanking God that he is alive".

May I quote from another article concerning a skydiver who survived after taking a two mile plunge from the sky. "Why didn't I die? I don't know. I remember seeing the trees from above, she said. I probably don't remember anything past somewhere like 500 or 1,000 feet. I don't think I blacked out, but I think your mind says, "Hey, you can't handle this, so we're not going to let you see it". "That was good".

We never know how much we need to be loved until we are.
— S. H. Dewhurst

One word in the English language which holds a lot of meaning is the word empathy. To what extent one is able to empathize with another depends upon many things. First of all, there has to be consideration and understanding. At the same time, we are speaking about being able to project our own thoughts, feelings, and imaginations into those of another. For the most part, this is impossible. To actually infuse with, and become part of another's mind and thinking is indeed difficult. Such action lies at the heart of judgement. Perhaps that is why we cannot really understand another.

By the same token, members of the human race are quite able to be aware of, and sensitive to the feelings and conditions of others. Such understanding is most helpful as well as meaningful at certain times. Let me outline the thinking of one individual who had recently gone through a serious accident that left him in a state of disarray.

Yesterday we spent some thirty minutes with a Doctor who specializes in restoring facial contours like mine, that have been mal-arranged because of illness or accident. The various components of change were reviewed. The placement of the eyebrows, the bony shapes under the skin, the outline of the chin, the angle of the jaw, the lack of proper lip contour, the position of the left eye, the presence of too much sclera showing etc...etc.

Obviously, proper changes will require months of work and healing. It at once becomes obvious that people who have not had to function like me, without being able to function, do not realize just how difficult it is to even get ready to go out in the morning. You are unable to shave. You can't really see very well, so it takes some 45 minutes to review the morning news. Everything you do seems to take twice as long. The cereal must be mixed twice, heated in the microwave, and then strained before you are able to absorb it between the plates and wires that cover the front of the mouth.

Still, life goes on. Yesterday the city water meter inspector said it appears that you have a leak in your pipe somewhere. The amount of water being used is in excess of what is normal. A detective is required to determine not only the location, but also the required amount of work to correct the situation. Decisions have to be made at the office. Patients require attention. One realizes that he may never do dentistry again. Unless something is done soon, there will be no patients to treat. Their presence has much to do with the total value of any dental practice. A $900 appraisal is required to establish a value prior to advertising. One needs to stop and consider the words of Bern Williams, "Hope for perfection, but don't scorn improvement".

Until you look in the mirror and see a totally different face than you used to look at, you failed to realize just how devastating that can be. Those obvious scars on the check, missing teeth with wires holding the others together, eyes that peer out at different levels in the face, a tentative smile without real meaning, a chin that has different lengths, and more importantly, the inability to speak in any sort of coherent manner.

Have you ever walked down the street, and noted that people give you a wider berth simply because you look different? Only a few years ago you had dimples when you smiled. People generally considered you to be good looking. Of course, producing that deep gutteral sound when speaking has a certain undesirable connotation.

You find that your business is at a standstill, the roof leaks and the gas bill is due. Your employees need supervision as well as a salary, and you are unable to assist with any of the above. Why not contact your attorney and sue for $1 million? The wheels of justice do move slowly. Your time will come to present your case. Of course there is a good chance you wil be bankrupt by then.

"The trouble with many people who stop to count their blessings is that their arithmetic is so poor". — O.A. Battista. Despite the perils of life and living, there are many things to be thankful for. It is also true that some individuals seem to have more difficult problems than others. Still, challenges are necessary. They are always educational, and those things in which we participate will be remembered the best.

It has been said that hind sight is 20/20 vision. Taking a vantage point some six years after the event of misfortune helps one to see improvement. After all, one's physical health is better, the sun is still shining, and there is ample opportunity if one puts forth some effort. While his father died this spring at the ripe old age of 94, it is still worth remembering it was his donation of $5,000 that overcame some of the debts that had to be paid while one was recuperating.

Of course everything has been said that needs to be said. But
since no one was listening, it has to be said again — Unknown

There was a time in my life when everyone was listening, but me. This time was some 13 days after the accident. To me, this time was most unusual. I had never spent any real time in a hospital. Frankly, I was unaware that I was in a hospital. Where was I? It all depends upon what part of me you mean. No, I did not go through an out of body experience. Perhaps it could best be expressed as a sub-conscious body experience. Physically, I was there all right. Mentally, I was not.

When I finally looked in a mirror with my conscious mind, I simply asked, "Where am I? What happened?" Prior to that time I had been responding to questions asked, pin pricks and other sorts of stimulation. Still, none of it had registered with my conscious mind. No wonder I had requested that I be sent home every day. My subconscious self did not appreciate being restrained and kept inactive. I had things to do. Places to go, and people to see. I was like the traveling salesman; I had customers everywhere!

In retrospect, this condition was for my best good. I did not remember the accident itself. I did not suffer from any form of shock. After all, when looking at a picture of my face in the back seat of the Chrysler sedan, I could have gone into shock. As it was, I did not see anything, hear anything, and best of all, I did not feel anything. Nearly all of the bones in my face and jaws were either rearranged or fractured, except my nose. While my two front teeth were never found, the shape of my nose remained the same. Interesting.

During this time in the hospital, I lost some twenty pounds of both fat and muscle tissue. Yes, I was fed through a vein as well as through the wires that held my face together. Still, it required more calories to repair the damage than I received. I was attended hourly by fine medical personnel. If any of them were to walk through this room today, I would not recognize them. They did all they could for me. I sincerely appreciate their effort.

In learning about those 13 days of my life that were lost, I find I had more friends than I thought. Yesterday I reviewed some 88 cards and letters received during that time. It was most heartening indeed to hear about the daily phone calls and other acts of consideration and concern that were expressed in my behalf.

ONE MAN'S TRAGEDY

Life is filled with challenges. How and why they occur differs from person to person. There seems to be no general thread that follows such unfortunate events as accidents. Some would conclude they occur simply because you were in the wrong place at the wrong time. While this theme is associated with the events both before and after one man's tragic accident, it also spells out those things which also befell others who had close association with this victim.

Looking at the events of this story through the eyes of several individuals provides vantage points of interest. At the same time, the victim himself has a story to tell. After all, he did lose some 14 days of life. This does not mean he passed into another realm, but it does mean he lacked specific knowledge of what happened to him during that period of time.

Possibly the real tragedy involved the events that followed immediately after the victim returned home from the hospital and was faced with several important decisions. It became necessary to liquidate his ownership in an active dental practice as well as the real estate involved. A Corporation to which he belonged found it necessary to enter into a Chapter 7 bankruptcy. He was sued by two different individuals. He had never experienced this before. One of the lawsuits was won by the plantiff because of false documents presented to a Seattle Judge. Unfortunately the Judge decided the matter based on these documents. As a result, the victim was once again victimized and lost some $300,000 which constituted his life's savings. He went through the possibility of a personal bankruptcy, but decided that it would not happen.

Other events besides his need to recover from the injuries of an accident that could have led to death, included the loss of sizeable funds invested in three other business ventures. In addition, any funds received from insurance proceeds went to Blue Cross, attorneys, and the Resolution Trust Corporation. This is a story in itself.

How these events affected his wife and family as well as employees and friends rounds out the matter. Because of his need to work, he also faces discipline from the Dental disciplinary borard for providing services under the same roof as an unlicensed denturist. Several chapters have been started, and pretty well spell out the facts surrounding this American tragedy.

PAPERWORK, PAPERWORK, PAPERWORK

While the title of this particular section could lead one to believe we are speaking about governmental involvement, we are instead speaking about legal/insurance information. If any of you have ever given a deposition, you know what I mean. It takes a great deal of time, and oftimes the questions are repetitious and somewhat irritating.

Years ago, while stationed in west Germany after World War II, it was obvious the government there had a page or two for everything that happened. One could not add to his house without a permit, he could not even make sauerkraut in his basement without permission and that sort of intrustion entered into nearly everything that was done. It is not too different here in the good old USA today. The governmental requirements are far too involved in the affairs of the public.

In going through some papers I ran across an original copy of a deposition that was given to an attorney who flew to Seattle from Sacramento to take the statement from me some two years after the accident itself. It is obvious the insurance company concerned was delaying payment of its legal obligation just as long as possible. One of the main things they wished to do was to see just how well the patient had recovered from the accident. Should the matter go to trial, it would be in the best interests of the insurance company to demonstrate that the one person concerned was just as well physically and mentally two years after the accident as he was prior to the accident. The questions that were asked helped to make this point clear.

Another area of concern with the Insurance Company was whether or not me, the accident victim, was now making as much money as prior to the accident. If so, that would more or less prove the accident itself did not really injure me enough to prevent me from working. As a result a number of questions were asked to determine the truth of the matter.

The final area of concern was whether or not there were any physical impairments that would prevent me from doing my day to day activities in a somewhat lessened state. Here, since most of my injuries were above the neck, one could point to the chewing ability, the visual aquity and other facial features that were unusual or abnormal. "Are you able to eat a steak?", was one of the questions. "How far are you able to open your mouth?" Was another. "Does your deviated nasal septum cause any trouble?"

In summary then, a determination was made with regard to my physical, mental and financial well being. After that, negotiations were in order to close the matter.

"To the Light, my Lord and Savior Jesus Christ, to whom I owe all that I have. He is the Staff I lean on; without Him I would fail."
— Betty J. Eadie

In recent years we have heard much from those who profess to know more than the average about life after death. If we can believe their stories, they have experienced supernatural events which provide some added insight about life beyond the grave. One book, "Closer to the Light", was written by an MD, and recounts several experiences given by those with whom he has worked as they "opened their eyes after death". Another book entitled, "The Light Beyond", focuses in on experiences given by those who were militarily trained. In all instances, the influence of an immortal Being enters into the story as a source of blinding Light.

Were man to believe that he is composed of an earthly part, the body; and an eternal part, the spirit, that belief in and of itself would tend to influence his thinking here on earth. After all, the physical part is limited in its length of life.

If the spiritual part continues to exist, and later reunites with the resurrected physical part, that combination together eternally poses something that is worth looking towards.

For many years now, man has spoken about Heaven and Hell. Without getting into the specifics, neither future event seems to have done much to alter the life and activity of the majority of those who live on earth at the present time.

If an average issue of the National Enquirer represents today's man and woman, we are not making much progress towards eternal perfection. Take for example the comments of Loni Anderson concerning her former husband, Burt Reynolds. "With a gun in his hand, wildly jealous Burt, threatened to kill her if he caught her with another man". Yet, on a page written prior to this quotation, one Aaron Howell flatly turned down film makers who were hoping to rent his Iowa home as a movie set. The house was to be used to house a lonely farm wife who has a brief affair with a photographer. Mr. Howell would not stand for this kind of hanky-panky in his house. "There's a lot of things worth more in this world than money", stated the 84 year old homeowner.

Most of us agree with Frank Walsh who indicated that, "I never cease to be amazed at the strength of my weaknesses". Perhaps that is what Garth Brooks had in mind when he said "John Wayne's characters knew what was right and wrong, whether they were the good guy or the bad guy".

If we lose affection and kindness from our life, we lose all that gives it charm.
— Cicero

In a recent T.V. program, several men who were sentenced to die were interviewed. One 31 year old fellow indicated he had done nothing commendable during his entire life. He had been victimized by drugs and other fellows who led him in the wrong direction. In the end he killed a fellow human being, while robbing a bank.

Along with a recent article contained in the local newspaper was a picture of an injured man lying on the ground. He was obviously in pain, but was being administered to by two men from a local emergency unit. Standing in the background was an eleven year old boy with his hands on top of his head. He was obviously concerned about what he was witnessing. The injured person had been shot in the leg.

The article in question had the heading, *"Besieged by Crime!"* Tacoma is awash in violence. On the west coast, only Los Angeles and Oakland are more violent places to live. Our surge of crime is exacting a massive price, not just in social terms, but in economic costs as well. What went wrong to get us where we are today? And what's the solution?"

Having worked in downtown Tacoma for the past four years, a number of things stand out. Most of the patients that were treated in our office, were drug addicts. I suppose Tacoma General Hospital can say the same. We also saw many who were HIV positive. Most were also on welfare. Does this simple statement help to answer the question posed by the newspaper article? Certainly! Downtown societies have changed. Of course, out in the west part of town we read about gun carrying gangs who provide drive-by shootings on a regular basis.

Let me backtrack for just a moment. My reason for working in downtown Tacoma stemmed from my accident. Here was a job opportunity that did not require me to pay any of the normal office overhead. I was provided with a full time assistant as well as the necessary supplies and dental equipment. It appeared to be a sensible temporary location simply because it paid the mortgage as well as living expenses.

One dentist in downtown Tacoma lost his license for over-prescribing narcotics. This was easy to do. It was a daily concern. Unable to obtain the desired medication from the hospital, patients would fake a toothache in order to obtain the desired prescription. Time had to be spent in diagnosis that could be better spent in productive work. It became necesssary to refuse to write prescriptions for many who wanted the necessary relief.

Last year, 5,500 people in Tacoma and its suburbs were victims of violent crime. On the average, someone was raped, killed, robbed or assulted with a deadly weapon once every hour and a half. Over the past seven years, FBI statistics show Tacoma's homicide rate to exceed the national average for cities of a similar size by over 30%. This particular crime is the one that cannot be manipulated by differences in reporting practices. As a result, it does become a most sobering statistic.

Fortunately my four years in Tacoma did not lead to my becoming a local statistic. Still, it was obvious the people who worked there had become somewhat used to the situation and as a result, desensitized to much that occurred. In effect, they had become more hardened when it came to recognizing and reporting unlawful activity. At the same time, while there was no lack of local police in the area, there was obvious lack of crime control.

It has become apparent in our society that individuals who use drugs on a regular basis can all end up in a similar way. Basically, love of money lies at the root cause. If there was no demand for these things, the problem would be erradicated. It was my opinion years ago that Americans were too smart to become involved in these things. All such problems were limited to South

America. Obviously, I was wrong. Today we continue to build additional housing for criminals who then become non-productive members of society.

Still, in another way, this practioneer did become a statistic. There are, on the average, some 20 dentists that come under scrutiny each year by the state dental disciplinary board. This group acts pretty much on their own although they do use attorneys from the state Attorney General's office. They can become very vindictive at times. One attorney told me of a case where they spent untold hours putting together a case so the result would never be in doubt. In my own case it is obvious they have made the decision of "guilt by association" prior to reviewing any of the evidence.

Naturally there are legal ramifications involved. Here again, the under-signed did sign a document that has probably sealed his fate. Once again, he did not seek legal counsel prior to signing and misunderstood exactly what the document represented. Some of the following pages will help to clarify the matter. Time will tell what the final result will be. Usually it is loss of one's license and a monetary fine of some kind.

The vast majority of Americans have little use for law enforcement of any kind. True, they may receive a speeding ticket when they are caught in aradar trap, but other than that they have little to do with the various ramifications of the law. At the same time, we also recognize that we can be cited and charged with a lawsuit for one reason or another. Still, the majority of us are law abiding by nature, and are frankly appalled by the time and money we have to spend in order to deal with today's criminals.

One can only philosophize with regard to the reasons for today's criminal activity. Is it the age of abundance in which we live? Can the parents of today be blamed for the misdeeds of their children? Perhaps. After all, they have been spoiled. They have not needed to learn how to work. Respect for individuals on all levels is lacking. Home life is different today than it was in earlier times. Perhaps if we had to study by the light of a coal oil lantern, we would be less inclined to forget that educcation is not a right, but a priviledge.

One thing we cannot do is to close our eyes to what is happening on today's crime scene. Although we may dislike reading the paper, or watching the news on T.V., we cannot help but realize that society is over burdened by today's criminal element. Earlier some remarks were made with regard to the city of Tacoma in Washington state. Let me bring you up to date with regard to their budget problems because of their crime rate. In 1992, 24,485 crimes were committed in Tacoma. In 1993, that number increased to 25,940. This amounts to an additional 1,455 incidents. Most of this increase is due to aggravated assaults, car thefts, and residential burlaries. In effect, it amounts to a 5% increase in one year.

Of course the city of Tacoma has other problems in the budget as well. Their $16 million of increased spending is required in such things as an increase in health care and labor settlements. Revenue growth will likely cover half of this increase. As a result, it will be necessary to make some $8 million in cuts in order to balance the budget for next year. Of course this story is nothing new to the majority of our cities and states in this country. Nearly all of them are facing up to a shortfall when it comes to having enough money to fund all the programs.

This subject could be extended to mention an expected shortfall in necessary living expenses by those on welfare or Social Security. Is there any realistic approach to the conservative life style that was employed by both the founding fathers and the early American pioneers?

Strange things happen in the crime world today. Last week one person was killed when he was held by two men for taking one package of cigarettes from a local Safeway store. That death is now being ruled a homicide, and there will be an inquiry made. Today, the paper indicates a local 14 year old has been charged with stealing three packages of cigarettes from the same store. One would think he should think twice about doing such a thing. Still, most 14 year olds seldom read the daily news.

Two other articles tell about the activities of two twenty year olds. Both have been convicted of murder. One killed his 72 year old grandmother, the other was guilty of shooting another person when his attempt to sell drugs went awry. In the latter case, witnesses had been reluctant to testify because they feared death themselves. Other gang members had threatened to kill anyone who testified.

Approximately 80% of mothers get what is commonly called "baby blues" after giving birth. Usually this condition lasts only about two weeks. While this condition is thought to be triggered by hormonal changes, there are probably other personal conditions that enter in. Some 10% of the new mothers seem to develop a longer lasting condition known as postpartum depression. This condition seems to have some real physical connotations. Headaches, numbness, chest pains, and even despair and nightmares can enter in. As a result, as time goes on, feelings of suicide and anger towards the new child can occur. The family of a Federal Way woman who killed herself and her three children believes she suffered from many of these symptoms. A note that was written some 24 hours before she died mentioned that her boyfriend could not be made happy and dying was the only approach possible. Indeed this is sadly unfortunate.

After reading the "morning news", one could be led to believe everyone and everything is "going to hell in a handbasket", as someone has observed in times past. The unfortunate part of the five o'clock news today is that it seems to focus on these sort of events. After all, they are news, and reporters do need to report. Still, it is the impression of this writer that there are also many events happening that are never mentioned. These events can be described as uplifting, helpful, generous, useful, thoughtful, desirable, kind, but still uneventful.

Hopefully society at large is still able to avoid postpartum depression when it comes to the unfortunate happenings of the day. After all, life does go on, and it then becomes necessary to spend one's time trying to find something useful to do.

CHAPTER IV

"I don't think it's healthy for a young child to sit and watch killing on T.V." — James Jones, Father of Four

Back in August 1992, a family living in a remote section of Northern Idaho found it necessary to use weapons as they withstood the attack of Federal Marshalls for eleven days. Of course. Randy Weaver had been convicted earlier of a Federal weapons charge which he had not recognized personally. As a result, he was to be arrested.

When recently released from prison. Randy thanked the efforts of a well known attorney from Jackson, Wyo., as well as the American Justice system, which he had wished to disband earlier. As a white separist. Randy had reached a point in prison when he, "almost didn't care about winning his freedom." After all, he had lost his wife and one son during the standoff, and had also been responsible for the death of one U.S. Marshall. During his trial he was acquited of murder and conspiracy, but was convicted of lesser charges which led to 16 months in a Boise, Idaho prison.

One might ask a simple question, "Why has our society become so violent during the past twenty years?" Many answers have been provided. At the same time, it would appear we have reverted to the days of the outlaws when it was important to "shoot now and talk later". One of our earlier Presidents felt that it was important to walk softly, but to carry a big stick. Apparantly these thoughts have been renewed today.

Because of several unfortunate killlings this year just prior to Christmas, many law abiding citizens have demanded Federal action. As a result, we have seen gun enforcement laws go into effect. Of course, if guns are taken away from law abiding people, only the lawless will have guns. That would not be the right approach to the problem.

One survey indicates that some 54% of us believe that violence on T.V. contributes to violence in society. A Galiup poll taken last October would lead us to believe that 68% of the public consider T.V. violence to be a very important cause of crime throughout the country. This would no doubt make T.V. producers happy to know their medium has become so well watched. Could it also be that parents and teachers have neglected their responsibility in teaching our new citizens? Some 97% of us have concluded that lack of moral training in the home is a major factor in today's problem. In addition, lack of punishment by those who deliver punishment, as well as a poor quality of public education for our youth seem also to be responsible.

One may well ask the question, "Will we ever get away from the influence of violence in this country?" Based on what we see happening today the answer must be a resounding NO! Even now, in Memphis, Tennesee, we see another investigation concerning the REAL death of Martin Luther King. One Lloyd Jowers has recently disclosed that it was he who hired a killer to dispose of Mr. King. This means the 99 year sentence given to James Earl Ray was a mistake. In any event, the continual re-exploration of the deaths of John F. Kennedy as well as Martin Luther King will do nothing to restore their lives. Hopefully it may do something to set the record straight as well as to determine once and for all who was really responsible for these deaths.

Whatever the cause of past and present problems related to violence in this country, we still have a present day problem to solve relating to our youth. That problem centers around the presence of weapons of various kinds in our schools. Recently our state Superintendent of Public Instruction requested a mere $7 million to be used specifically to control this problem in one state. Just think how many textbooks that amount of money would buy! In fact, we could easily build another new high school somewhere.

Last year, it was reported from 219 of the state's 296 school districts that some 1,717 weapons incidents had occurred. Of that number, firearms were involved in 257 cases. Some 834 instances dealt with either knives or daggers. The remaining 834 happenings included the use of brass knuckles, nun-chee-ka sticks, throwing stars, clubs, the use of screwdrivers, and razor blades. Admitedly this kind of activity can be seen on most T.V. stations at nearly any time of the day or night.

It was Norman Vincent Peale who observed that "Your world, the worldyou live in day by day, is just about what you make it. It will be no better or bigger or finer than you are yourself". Someone else has observed that America will be strong so long as she is good. Indeed, "Each of us will one day be judged by our standard of life - not by our standard of living; by our measure of giving - not by our measure of wealth; by our simple goodness — not by our seeming greatness". — Ohio Mason

**Violence Comes in Different Ways and Kinds, BUT the
Result is always the same: Sorrow for someone. — Anon.**

It really doesn't matter too much whether or not it is a drunk driver in a 4X4 or a gun toting teenager, when loosed on society, someone is going to suffer as a result. For example, there is the "special needs" car seat that was invented to carry someone in a cast in the back seat of an automobile. It was designed especially for the youngster who weighs under 40 pounds, but who was, or is wearing a body cast. Obvously that individual requires special care in a special kind of car seat. This seat cost someone $130, but that someone has donated the seat to the Safety Restraint Coalition to be passed around for the benefit of others.

After some twelve days in the hospital, Bobby Hurley left in a wheel chair. The article did not say how many pounds he had lost. He was wearing dark glasses, a cast on his right leg, and a sling holding his left shoulder in place. He is the professional basketball player who was thrown from his truck because he was not wearing a seat belt. It is thought he will play very little basketball for twelve months.

We would never leave the ground in a single engine airplane unless everyone aboard was wearing a seat belt. It is not normal to wear a seat belt. In fact, it does not become a habit for three weeks. After that the driver and others concerned simply put the belt on automatically. This is one kind of present that will continue to give after the holidays.

Court records show that on the evening of March 24th, Gaitan was drinking vodka, and Ramos was smoking marijuana when they decided it was time for action. At that point they should have been inactivated. What happened next is considered to be one of the worst crimes known to police in the vacinity of Yakima, Washington. Their victims were all white, and were little known in the neighboring town of Outlook, where they had moved two years ago from Fresno, California. No motive was ever established for the crime. Apparently it was committed simply to steal a few personal belongings, which they could use later to brag about the event. In short, all four members of the Micheal Skelton family were clubbed and beaten to death by the two fourteen year olds.

How would you like to hit some "black ice", and find yourself some 80 feet off the highway into a cold river where your car filled with water? This happened to four members of the Eggleston family on one chilly winter day. Fortunately rescuers were not far away, so three members were quickly rescued. Unfortunately the father of the family lost his life. Yes, there are various forms of violence, but sorrow always results for someone.

We were writing about violence in our society. Every morning when I bring in the paper, my wife says she does not want to hear anything about the news before breakfast. Of course, one could also say, not only the newpapers, but also the news on T.V. is enough to take away one's appetite.

"A 23 year old Tacoma woman was out for a walk Sunday morning near Wright Park. She was abducted, raped, robbed and stabbed". These sort of things used to be somewhat common in large eastern cities. Today they seem to happen everywhere. For your information, Wright Park is in the Northeast part of the city up on the hill. Only two blocks away is Tacoma General Hospital in one direction, and a city high school in the other direction. This is not considered to be the most dangerous part of Tacoma.

"The woman was walking along Division Avenue when a man approached her on the sidewalk. The man grabbed the woman and took her to a nearby home. There she was raped, and her purse was stolen". After this illegal and immoral action, the same woman was taken to the 300 block of North K Street, where she was stabbed several times in the upper body". Sometime later, a private security guard from some nearby building found the victim at 4:18 a.m. She was still alive, so was taken a few blocks by ambulance to the nearby hospital. Her condition was considered to be stable.

It is interesting to read about the description of the man who was described as the assailant (perhaps the word assassin is better). He was said to be 20 years old, (how could one know?) He was about 5 feet 10 inches tall, and of medium build, whatever that means. His clothing was dark blue and black. Somewhere a white logo was seen. Not too helpful. In fact, the race of the individual is never mentioned. No wonder these kind of criminals are seldom found. But then today, one must never incriminate another on the basis of race, sex, religion or age.

While this treatise makes no claim to understand the mind of anyone, it is obvious that times are far different than when He, the writer was growing up. He notes with sorrow that the state of California has nearly 115,000 people in jail today. Each one costs the taxpayers some $25,000 annually to maintain. The biggest complaint from the prisoners is that they learn nothing useful while in prison. Nothing useful that could quality them for a job on the outside. In addition, nearly 50% of these prisoners are returned for a second or third semister. It would be cheaper if we were to send them to college outside the prison system. Never give in, never, never, never, never in nothing, great or small. NEVER give in except to convictions of honor and good sense — Sir Winston Churchill

While it is not the intent of this person to dwell on the cause of, or the result of accidental injury, it is not difficult for one to pontificate with regard to those activities entered into by men and women which can be classified as dangerous in the extreme. Of course we must admit that what is dangerous to one person is not so to another. Some people would never consider sky diving or para-gliding. At the same time, others would never swim with sharks or care to drive race cars.

Frequently in the news these days we read about individuals who do things that would not be considered sensible to others. At times, we also read that those individuals end up with accidental injury. "Ricky and Ernie had been running nose to tail; then Ernie dropped off a bit. It looked as if Ernie then went straight into the wall without scrubbing any speed off at all. The car went up on its left side so high, I could see the star on the hood. I knew it was a violent hit". So stated Ricky Rudd's crew chief. Bill Ingle, who was sitting atop a transporter in the garage area, acting as spotter during the practice session that led to the injury of Ernie Irvan.

"Irvan's brain and lungs suffered the brunt of the blow", doctor Errol Eriandson said in an afternoon news conference. "Also, the driver's skull was fractured at its base, and his brain stem suffered severe swelling". Presently Irvan is breathing only with the help of a respirator, and is under constant monitoring.

Last week, someone interviewed a hydroplane driver on T.V. At the time, he was in a bed in the local hospital. Everything seemed to be going along fine until a gust of wind began to lift the nose of the ship. The driver acknowledged at that point his control over the hydroplane was gone. Review of the photographs indicated the ship went up into an almost verticle position, and then the front end slammed down hard onto the water, breaking off the front end which then skidded ahead of the rest of the boat. As a result, both legs of the driver were fractured, and other internal injuries also resulted. It appeared he was on the way to a satisfactory recovery however.

Perhaps it is best to be philosophic rather than distressed. As Joe Lewis indicated, "Every man's got to figure to get beat sometime".

EMPATHY

As we review historic events, or human events of many kinds, we find it helpful to thank a Divine source that we were not involved. None of us has any desire to suffer unnecessarily as we travel along our course of life. It is always nice to travel as simply and as happily as possible.

Since none of us can avoid unfortunate happenings entirely, the time arises when we must learn how to empathize with someone else. In other words, we develop the capacity to participate in another's feelings or ideas. Naturally we are unable to do this without knowledge. Knowledge of circumstances pertaining to the surroundings which were in force at the time of the trial. In addition, few of us have learned how to read another's mind. As a result, we sometimes tend to over exaggerate or to over simplify another's thoughts and/ or feelings.

Recently I came across a letter written by my wife to her mother. The date was 6 May 1988. Knowing this was day six after the accident, and that I was lying in the intensive care unit at the Chico Hospital, it was interesting for me to catch up on my wife's feelings and thoughts at a time when my conscious self was lying unconscious.

Since the letter was short, (she called it a quick note) it became necessary to read between the lines. There was obvious concern expressed. Concern for the future status of the undersigned. In fact, the final statement reads, "Must go back to see Ralph". At the same time, other parts of the letter expressed other feelings. Thanks was given for financial aid, as well as for those phone calls received which helped to provide support for those who suffered. Another expression said, "Your thoughts and prayers are HERE with us. That helps alot."

For several days now, the patient had been difficult to relate to. Not only because his teeth were wired shut, but because he seemed somehow, to be far far away. The oral surgeon in charge had tried to explain exactly what was wrong. The patient still wanted to return home. He had important things to do. The fact that it would take another eight weeks for him to heal properly seemed not to be recognized.

According to his wife's letter, the patient had always been active and alert. Patiently waiting, had never been one of his virtures. At the same time, it was not known until one week later that his mental self had been on vacation as well. On the 13th day after the accident, he looked into the mirror and asked,

"Where am I?" "What happened?" At that time, it was obvious he had discovered a new and different period had arrived in his life.

Another interesting thought appears in the wife's letter. The writer admits to having a few "down times" now and then. It would appear that her concern for the patient's condition was the main reason. She indicated there appeared to be a certain amount of progress each day. As a result, she expressed thanks and happiness when it was evident. In addition, a heartfelt feeling of love and affection towards all who had tried to help during these difficult times is mentioned. Cards and letters were received along with well meaning telephone calls.

In retrospect, one senses his inability to fully empathize with another person without being able to put their thoughts together completely. By the same token, it is always interesting to try. Whenever one loses a week or two of life, he can't help but wonder what others around him knew, and were doing and thinking in relation to his condition. Hence, the reason for this particular writing.

There is a rather critical test for those who lie in bed incapacitated in one way or another. If they are able to remove the childproof cap from the medicine bottle in the first try, then they are not as sick as they thought they were.

SEEING IS BELIEVING

According to the Medical Dictionary, a sense is a faculty by which the conditions or properties of things are perceived. This definition tends to cover certain medical territory that is unfamiliar to most of us. We think in terms of special senses. Seeing, feeling, hearing, tasting and smelling.

One might well ask, what is the most important sense? In the absence of a scientific survey, most of us would select the sense of sight. The least important sense would probably be the sense of smell. Of course the act of seeing itself, has several areas of interest. One can be near sighted, far sighted, short sighted, long sighted, day sighted, night sighted, or even old sighted. All of these separate catagories constitute an area of medicine known as Opthalmology.

In years gone by, the term oculist was used to describe a medical specialist who focused in on vision as a field of endeavor. Today that term is both inadequate and incomplete. Referring once again to the Medical Dictionary shows two full pages of words which pertain to vision and its several sub-headings.

Most of us take visual health for granted. While we may have an annual eye exam, and correct our lenses as required, unless something unusual happens, we forget there can be some undesirable things that lurk in the shadows of sight. Today's surgery for cataracts is both fast and painless. But, what about something that cannot be easily seen by the human eye?

Recently, this writer went through a diagnosis which was somewhat more involved. He was examined by three or four eye doctors who seemed to be puzzled by his condition. Disappointment set in when three of the four suggested that he have cataracts removed. When one's eye is changing in position, and double vision sets in, it is time for another opinion. Cataracts were not the problem. In fact, they did not exist.

Fortunately we do live in a time when a proper diagnosis of most illnesses is possible. All one needs to do is to find the right person, and then combine his knowledge with the right equipment. In this instance, that information was found at the university eye center. Here, a series of magnetic resonance images were obtained. These words are not to be found in *Dorland's Medical Dictionary* dated in 1951. The MRI machine is something of recent vintage. It does not use X-rays to diagnose the problem. In fact, it emits a radio frequency which interacts with the hydrogen atoms in the tissue. Bones do not interfere with this image, and tissue sections as thin as 0.7 millimeters can be secured. These fine cross sections can be most useful in diagnosing the problem.

The MRI sections in my case showed a definate growth between the floor of the left orbit and the eyeball. Because of a continued displacement of the eye over time, it was obvous this growth was active. The indicated solution for me was surgery.

While no one likes to go under the knife, at times it can be mandatory. Fortunately for us, we soon become unaware of time as well as the procedure being performed. Being rendered unconscious with today's medical technology certainly beats receiving a blow on the head.

In my own case, some 2 1/2 hours of surgery went by without my knowledge. The big question arose later when my mind once again became conscious. After all, most physicians are trained to portray a "worst case senario" when talking about surgical results in advance. This meant the tumor to be removed could be cancerous. It also meant the optic nerve could be involved, and could also be lost along with the sight of one eye. The unknown is always a frightening thing to contemplate.

A third surgeon was also standing by to secure some bony chips from my skull to fill in the floor of the orbit should that be found to be necessary. He later told me his services were not required, for which I was most thankful. The results themselves would need to be given the test of time. An eye bandage was applied, and when it was removed two days later, eyesight seemed to be normal. While none of us has control over every event that happens in life, Bern Williams had the right suggestion when he observed - "Time, the currency of our lives, is too precious to spend on brooding".

IS THIS MY DAY?

We all like to hear a happy ending to any venture or adventure. During the past ten years this writer has been one of millions who has returned entries for one contest or another. Nothing of any consequence has ever come of it until today.

Mr. Dick Clark who is one of Santa's elves along with Ed McMan, would like to meet with me in Salt Lake City, Utah on 1 Nov. At that time I am to present them with a cashier's check in the amount of $5,000. That check is to be exchanged for a check from them in the amount of $95,000. Why is this you ask? I am one of those preliminary winners of $100,000 who is also entered in the final contest for the $10 million prize. Here the odds are only 5,000 to one.

Exciting as this possibility is, it does tend to make one reminisce somewhat about life's happenings during the past ten years. As part of this small book herein presented, it does serve as a final chapter with a happy ending.

At the same time, I was also excited once before when I was chosen to be the final bidder on a $2 million apartment property in St. George, Utah. There were 15 bidders for this property which was in the hands of the Resolution Trust Corp. who liquidated many such properties across the country. Why was my bid accepted? One could say that it was pure luck just like the above presentation. Still, I did have three sources of funding who claimed to be able to pay cash for the purchase price. That seemed to make a difference to the RTC.

Like many of my other business ventures during the past ten years, the necessary funding failed to materialize. As a result, I lost some $100,000 of my own money. No one else was involved. This was one project that I had backers behind my backers, so I thought. At least I did spend untold hours of time and effort to bring this purchase about.

We won't take time to say anything about my losses in Anchorage as well as in Idaho and Nevada, (mining ventures). Still, life does have a way of heading on down the road whether we have a good vehicle to ride in or not. When a certain judgement went against me in court because a partner had me sign my life away, I thought my financial days were over. Fortunately I did avoid going bankrupt. Perhaps it is well to remember that we should not judge a man by what he drives, but by what drives him.

CONCLUSIONS

All of us have been victims of one scam or another. Recently this writer received a cashier's check on the amount of $46,500. There was no sender shown, only a bank in Iowa that had issued the check. In order to find out more, I went to my local bank and asked the manager to contact the bank in Iowa to determine where the check came from. This he was able to do. In effect, the check was a forgery that had been issued to someone else who had already negotiated it some time earlier. The check was returned to the Iowa bank together with some information pertaining to the person who had called me earlier on the phone with regard to sending me some funds. He did call back, and when I told him the check was not negotiable, he simply said, "It appears that our accounting department made a mistake". Since then, there has been no further contact.

Most of my calls have come from people in Canada who seem to have potential phone numbers of citizens of the USA who might respond to some kind of scam artist. So far, I have been able to side step them and their activities with no loss of funds. This has not always been possible in other business ventures. References to the material contained in the Appendix of this writing may be of interest in that regard.

One is reluctant to say that all phone calls asking for money or a credit card number are simple hoaxes. Still, it would appear that most of them do fit into that category. Once your card number has been found by some scam artist, it is well to change the card. This has happened to most of us at one time or another. In my case, I should have always followed the advice given to me by my father years ago. He indicated that it was never wise to give your money to someone else to invest. After all, you could make the same mistakes as that person. In case the money were to be lost, you would then have no one to blame but yourself.

It has been my conclusion in life that it is better to learn the trade than it is to learn the tricks of the trade. While many individuals do go through life thinking that the world owes them a living, it is still much better to make things happen through your own efforts. Along the way, one also develops some talents that may have been lying dormant. There may be times when we conclude that no one seems to care about our financial posture except us. That is never true. All we need to do is fail to file an annual income tax return, and we will soon find out who is still very much concerned.

APPENDIX

FORWARD

What is it that lies at the heart of many problems in society today? In a word, that thing is DISHONESTY. We are all aware of the recent demise of Enron for example. While the legal matters associated with this death will take years to resolve, there is no doubt but what it might have continued to be a successful corporation had its leaders been completely honest.

The *KIPLINGER LETTER* makes an interesting observation in its 22 Feb. issue. "Dishonesty is no more common in business than in any other fields. Or more common than among average citizens in their daily lives, where there's a lot of lying, tax evading, shoplifting, welshing on debt. This is a challenge for ALL of society....demphasizing winning at any cost and elevating fair play, honesty and compassion for others".

What we seem to be thinking here is that man is no more moral. If all of us were taught to be strictly honest at our mother's knee, this kind of society would probably not exist. This is not to criticize our mothers. They probably did the best they could while trying to work outside the home as well as inside. Needing to leave their children for someone else to raise can lead to a total lack of proper instruction when it comes to dealing with one's fellowmen.

We have all heard that, "honesty is the best policy". Most of our businesses try to follow that principle. At the same time, it has become very much to the forefront that this idea must have passed its time. If not so, why so much dishonesty today? Have we really found anything better?

Yes, mothers and fathers may be somewhat to blame. Is it not in the home where we really learn our most important social contacts? Is it not there where we should hear about Christian principles? We later learn that lying, stealing, cheating, and fornication are common expressions of "other" people's life style. When we stop and think about it, we probably heard something about those things years ago. If not, what does our conscience say? If that part of our mental make-up is absent, we need to go back and find out why.

We will find in this reading that the white man's scalp is there for the taking. Those who make it their life's work soon find out who they may take advantage of. It is easy for them to determine exactly who is an easy mark. After all, experience has shown them who this is.

IF YOU VALUE YOUR REPUTATION,
GUARD YOUR ACTIONS
IF YOU PRIZE YOUR FRIENDSHIPS,
BRIDLE YOUR TONGUE.
— William Arthur Ward

One of the most chilling experiences in life is to find oneself in a room filled with husbands and wives, all of whom are business partners of yours, then to learn they have met to criticize you, and to blame you for their business misfortune. One thing is for sure, the most sensitive nerve in the human body is the pocketbook.

After five years working as the managing partner for this unthankful group, they had met to decide whether or not a certain offer for the business was to be accepted. But, let's go back a few years. At that time, this same group met to decide if they should sink funds into several apartment properties in Anchorage, Alaska. The oil pipeline had been built and those who came to Anchorage to work had, for the most part departed. All Anchorage apartment properties were for sale at a reduced price since nearly 33% of the residents had gone to the lower 48. Still, a decision to purchase had been made, and the actual business of caring for the properties fell into my hands.

A Seattle attorney had been hired to draw up a partnership agreement. In hind sight, it turned out to be the wrong kind of partnership agreement, but no one in our medical field recognized that fact at the time. Basically the selling price was right, and all of us had a certain amount of the gambling urge with which to deal.

For several years I had been studying to obtain my real estate license. An interest in this field of endeavor seemed to urge me on. As the managing partner, I could charge the group less than any local management firm, and save all of us some money. At the same time, it gave me an opportunity to practice some of the things I had learned over the years. All in all, it appeared to be beneficial for all concerned.

All medical doctors and dentists soon realize the only way to really become proficient in their profession is to practice. While school may provide much knowledge, every case is different, and it simply takes experience in order to become trained. So it was with the apartment business as well. Working with people, banks, carpenters, roofers, tenants, agreements, suppliers, accountants, and painters was all very interesting. Over the following years, I was able to write an acceptable manual for all activities which we encountered. Things went well for the most part, and one on-site manager named her child after me.

Prior to THE meeting, the properties in question had been sold four times. Each time the price was too low to be acceptable. This was the fifth time around. The buyer had been able to get into the project with nothing down. He claimed good credit. It later proved to be otherwise. Still, the right time to sell had passed, and we were hoping to come out even with this new offer. Of course things never work out that way. Everyone was upset. One partner had brought his attorney along. He semed to focus in on my part in the proceedings accusing me of being misleading

Citizens in Alaska have benefitted over the years from receiving some $1,000 each year as part of the oil royalties. This seemed now to be insufficient to keep them there. Many moved to the lower forty-eight. Others found that work was hard to find. Homes went back to the banks, and apartment rentals declined drastically. Such were the economics of the time. We found that we owned an alligator. This is a beast that needs to be fed after the mortgage is paid. Since the mortgage was not getting paid, the beast became hungry, or in other words, we got deeper in debt.

Obviously it is always impossible to please those who have their minds made up. There is a statement that has been commited to memory on this subject: "When you're forming your opinion, do it carefully, go slow. Hasty judgements are followed by regretting, that I know. And in arguments, be careful, not too quickly to decide. Try to look upon the subject from the other fellow's side". The final decision would be that I would produce a final report within two weeks time, or I could expect to face a lawsuit. After all, someone had to be blamed.

Although it became necessary to return the properties to the banks concerned, my report seemed to satisfy the group. Still, there was no thanks ever forthcoming to me for selling the properties four times without charge. Greed had taken over. Money had been lost, but experience had been acquired. As Mr. Jesse Andrews observed, "Nothing makes a person work like being debt propelled".

What then did we learn? In a word, the answer is timing. There is a time to buy, and a time to sell. This timing is lost whenever greed enters in. It can also be lost when one waits too long.

It could well be that the reader has no interest in the intracacies of real estate. Either this subject could be foreign to his mind, or he could feel that it is a subject that should be discussed only between those who are in this form of business. Still, all of us are very much aware that one's single largest investment is usually his home. As a result, it behooves all of us to give some thought to the fundamental principles that underly what we own. Of course, big money can be involved. Real estate has led to more millionaires in this country than any other business.

Despite the fact that underlying all is the land, something else is even more important. That thing is money. Without proper financing, nothing will happen. Most small businesses in this country fail because of simple lack of sufficient capitol. One can never have too much in reserve.

It seems to be easy for those in this country who labor in the financial markets to make promises to their clients. One of their purposes is to encourage others to borrow. Unless they do, the broker as well as the lender will have no income. Unfortunately all borrowers have long since concluded that it is impossible to bank a promise. For some reason it is not accepted. One also learns that promises are free.

This writer has learned the hard way that even though he may provide his hard earned funds as an "up front" fee, and have a signed agreement as well, even that combination will not guarantee funding. Recently he had all these things in place, and still failed to fund a certain real estate project. Why? Because he was dealing with a crook! This person had no intention of producing and shortly before "funding" he demanded an additional $5,000 to "visit the site". It was not in the contract. He walked away with some $15,000 cash and seemed to have no conscience at all. Unfortunately this is not something that happens rarely. It is much too common in the USA today! All that one can do "after the fact", is to hire an attorney and hope that he may find some way to recover.

Another unfortunate thing today is that it is impossible to count on any Federal or state office to help. It is also difficult to find anyone who knows how to collect funds from individuals who have gone to another state or who have hidden their assets. Sometimes one simply has to say, "Let God judge between me and thee". Punishment for wrong doing is not always achieved in mortality. This does not mean that we should never trust our fellowman, but it does mean that we need to be more careful now than we did some fifty years ago, when a man's word was his bond, and a handshake was all that was needed to seal the deal.

> No one is more definate about the solution than
> the one who doesn't understand the problem. — Robert Half

Why do business deals go sour? Who is to blame? In what way does human nature enter in? After years of trying to make something good happen, yours truly has become an expert in these things. This does not mean he will no longer attempt to do any business. What it does mean is that he will try harder to avoid such things as being greedy, seeing a return in advance, believing in the long term prognostications of the broker, and being swayed by expert salesmanship. Of course, the latter talent is oftimes difficult to avoid.

It was Bert Murray who said that salesmanship is, "the art of the uninteresting made irrestible". It was nearly one year ago that this definition was applied to me. One day I was invited out to lunch by two reputable local businessmen. One was an accountant whom I had known for over twenty years. The other was an associate attorney who had just opened a local office. The object of my free lunch was an effort on their part to convince me that I should write a check for $12,500. At the time, bank accounts were paying some 2% on funds deposited. They were offering me a 15% annual return. In addition, I could also become a participant in future profits from the business that was forming, which participation amounted to some 2% of all profits. It sounded like one of those "ground floor opportunities".

Exactly which "hot buttons" had they pushed on my panel? One could simply say that if we risk a little to gain a lot, that makes good sense. At the same time, it is well to remember that if something sounds too good to be true, it usually is. At any rate, the $12,500 went into the attorney's trust fund, and an agreement was signed with an unknown Corp. President as well as thaccountant.

Since the six month due date has long since passed, this account along with others has been assigned to a collection agency. I am told the accountant is now threating to go bankrupt, and that suing a Corporation with no assets is less than useless. Meanwhile the attorney is home free because his trust fund was used only as a holding pen.

At this point it would be easy to point out that I only got what I deserved for being both greedy as well as naive. Perhaps so. At least the time comes when one must accept responsibility for his acts. Still, one likes to think that there are still a few honest businessmen left.

After being set-up, taken advantage of, used and abused, or in other ways defrauded, one is quite able to accept a statement made some time ago by Mr. Aterberry, of the U.S. Dept. of Justice. "Man's ability to work a fraud on his fellow man is infinite". Another thought that bears consideration is one that was made by Orson Pratt, "To take the advantage of a good man, and cheat him out of his property is an evil recognized by the consciences of all men. The inherent nature of such things is vicious". And so, we do have food for thought.

Yesterday I received a long distance phone call from Dallas, Texas. It was a local attorney who had a message to deliver. In recent days he had been in contact with "my man in Dallas" who was there to put a lien on a certain bank account as based on a judgement that has been in limbo for some time. The reason for the call was to let me know there would be no funds available to deliver to me. He represented others who had been swindled by the same person. As a result, they held a prior claim to any funds that might be available. While this news was something less than gleeful for me, it did point out a fact that I had known for some time. While some leopards may be able to change their spots, this one has never bothered to do so. When asked certain questions under oath, the defendant took the fifth amendment statement some 37 times according to the attorney concerned.

Going back a few years, the above named person contacted me by telephone. Perhaps I should have notified the Inspector General. At any rate, this person needed sizeable funds in order to get everything together to begin gold mining in the Yukon. Yes, this in and of itself is a red flag. Still, I did know something about mining, so I did listen to his approach.

No, I did not have sizeable funds, but I knew someone who did. At least he did have crediblity with the bank. After the three of us signed the bank note for $200,000 I was told these funds would not have been applied for if I did not sign. I had been checked out to determine whether or not I had sufficient assets to pay this sum back if the venture itself failed to do so.

As time went on, it became more and more obvious that this was another business venture that would go sour. The miners in the Yukon had no trouble spending all the money. They did, for some reason, find it difficult to return even one dollar after the season was over.

> The man who trusts men will make fewer mistakes than
> he who distrusts them. — Camillo Di Cavour

Most Americans are trusting people. This statement of fact may be less true today than it was some fifty years ago. While growing up, it seemed never to be necessary to lock one's home while gone on a two or three day trip. The door was always left open if the family was gone for only one day. Today, we are bombarded by advertising that would lead one to believe nothing is safe either inside the house or out. Hopefully that is not true in all locations.

While attending the Olympic games in Mexico City in 1968, we found ourselves surrounded by "shoe shine" boys. As a result, I sat down on a park bench and had my shoes shined. After paying the young man, we left the bench on foot. After taking a few steps, it became apparent that I had left my binoculars behind. Upon turning around, it was evident there were neither binoculars or boys to be seen. At the time, we thought this would never happen in the USA.

May I call your attention to the document on the following page. After you read it, I suspect you will! have some question concerning its contents. That statement was presented to me one morning together with a carrot and a stick. The carrot was that if I signed this paper, I would be eligible to participate in a sizeable sum of money that would be received from the sale of a Canadian mining property as well as the corporation which owned it. If I did not sign, I would then need to come up with $100,000 to help defray an existing bank note that three partners had signed. Since it was presented to me by one of the three partners, I had confidence that it would work out as stated, and so I signed it without advice of an attorney.

As time went on, the business itself deteroriated. One partner in Canada spent all the money. The other partner got me to sign the note which I later found out obligated me for the full $300,000 that had been borrowed. The judgement against me resulted from my signature on the following page. If there was any moral aspect to the law, that was never mentioned. I was called in and had to divulge my entire history to an attorney hired by my partner. After three hours, he knew more about my financial status than my banker.

The only recourse I had was a commercial piece of property on a corner which my partner had his eye on. As a result, he was willing to accept this in leiu of a cash payment. In addition he also became a partner with three other men who had been difficult for me to work with in trying to develop the site. The only good thing about the whole matter was that these four individuals deserved each other.

Earlier mention was made of the carrot and the stick. Because it was my opinion that I was being given correct information, I did sign the following document without my attorney's approval. Should you have a glimmer of understanding when you read it through, it would indicate to me that you have had some pretty extensive legal training.

I, ________, do hereby acknowledge notice of the assignment from Seattle First National Bank to ____________, of that certain debt evidenced by a promissory note, secured by a UCC Security agreement, both dated 12 May 1986, wherein 5714 Yukon Ltd., a Canadian Corporation is Maker/Debtor and Seattle First National Bank is Payee/Secured Party, and of my general guaranty agreement dated 12 May 1986, guarantying the above obligation, and do hereby consent to the assignment of the note, security agreement and my personal general guaranty to _________.

I acknowledge this Notice and Consent, both on behalf of myself individually and on behalf of 5714 Yukon, Ltd., in my capacity as Sectry/Treas.

Dated this _____day of _______ 1986.

____

My Signature

While some may conclude that the above transaction appears to be innocuous in content, most of us would automatically shy away from it simply because we do not understand either the language or its possible ramifications. According to one judge in summary judgement, by signing this document, I immediately exposed myself to a debt approximating $300,000. This turned out to be the single biggest financial mistake of my life.

After signing the above "guarantee of payment", the time did come when I had to pay. Fortunately it did not lead to a Chap. 7 bankruptcy. My attorney did his best in court. Later he sent me a letter which outlines his feelings on the matter. It comes under the title of Trujillo & Peick, P.S.

Yes, it is possible to shed many tears as we travel through life. Still, I believe that each of us must accept responsibility for our acts, right or wrong! Unfortunately, Mr. Aterberry makes sense when he said, "Man's ability to work a fraud on his fellowman is infinite".

December 1, 1988

Dr. Ralph G. Willie
30317 - 16th Ave. S.
Federal Way, WA 98003

        RE: vs. Willie
             Our File No. 20.9400.01

Dear Dr. Willie:

When I spoke with you on the phone last Tuesday, the news I had to deliver was some of the most unpleasant I have ever had to relay. The blow was not softened by the fact that I have consistently recommended from the beginning that we would lose this case. Being legally correct did not diminish my sympathy for you or your position.

I have enclosed a copy of the Order of Summary Judgment in this case. The order was granted by Judge Liem Tuai on November 22, 1988. It appeared clear he had his mind pretty well made up when we began the argument, since he asked counsel for only one brief question and then grilled me on several subjects. I will discuss those in this letter.

The Summary Judgment Order speaks for itself. Judgment is awarded on the principal amount of the note, plus attorney's fees and costs. The amount of interest is not subject to dispute, since it is a calculation. I did strenuously dispute the amount of attorney's fees, but the court chose to award the full amount requested. Frankly, the amount requested is pretty much reasonable.

As you remember, you signed a Note and Guarantee to Seattle First National Bank. While we may have some defenses to the Guarantee, including fraud at the inception and the like, we had no defenses to the Note. Since the Note was assigned to   he is entitled to collect on it. This is the point the court focused on. Frankly, I do not think this point is assailable on appeal.

You have a right to appeal this judgment. The appeal must be filed within thirty (30) days from the signature of the summary judgment order. That means it must be filed before Christmas. The cost of an appeal would be approximately $3,500.00-$5,000.00 for attorney's fees.

I am not confident we would win on the appeal. Further, to

prevent execution on the judgment, we would have to put up a bond
which would equal the amount of the judgment plus interest and
additional attorney's fees that would accrue before the decision
on the appeal.   Therefore, we would probably have to obtain a
bond in the amount $300,000. Normally, bonding companies would
require collateral for that amount equal to the amount of the
bond, or more.

_______ also indicated a willingness to work this out. I do
not know what that means, but I presume he still wants your
Federal Way property.

I would immediately consult with Mr. O'Rourke, or a competent
bankruptcy attorney, to consider your options. If you do not
have a good bankruptcy attorney, I would consult with Mr. Norman
Leopold, at 455-0555, (U.S. Bank Plaza, Bellevue, Washington).
Mr. Leopold is excellent in matters of this kind, and he is
absolutely trustworthy.

I would talk to a bankruptcy attorney before I made any decisions
on my future.   I would do so immediately, since we have only a
short period of time in which to consider an appeal.

While we both think that you were lead down the garden path in
this case, my objective legal opinion is that you are stuck
legally, despite the equitable arguments we might have. Since we
did not have an adequate opportunity to review this paperwork
before you signed it, you could not have gotten advise as to its
consequences then.   In the future, an attorney should review all
such legal paperwork before you sign it.   If this firm had been
consulted before the Note was signed we would have pointed out
the dangers of such an arrangement: dangers with which you are
now intimately acquainted.

On the other hand, we tried our very best to find an avenue of
defense.   We successfully held off Mr. _________ for over a
year, but in the end, I believe the decision of the court in this
case was legally, if not morally, correct.

Please see a bankruptcy attorney as soon as possible, and advise
me within a week of your intentions regarding appeal.

                              Best Regards,

                              TRUJILLO & PEICK, P.S.

                              Ralph W. Anderson

RWA:ja

JUSTICE ONCE AGAIN

When a new deputy Sheriff asked a female stage coach passenger who fired the shot that killed a male passenger, he opened a can of worms. Later, the two men who held up the stage were jailed, but also acquitted. They had not killed the passenger. That shot had come from a different source up on a nearby ridge.

Meanwhile, back in town, the rich miner's daughter hired two gunslingers to keep the peace. It was one of them who had fired the fatal shot from the ridge. Of course this was unknown to the deputy at the time. At the same time, the female passenger did know who he was, as she had been married to one of his friends.

As the senario unfolded, the town's citizens finally supported the deputy against a group of outside rough riders. One of the two gun slingers killed the other one while he was drunk. Since he was the person who shot the male passenger from the ridge, justice had been done. Of course movies do revolve around a plot of some kind, and at times we wish that we too could be part of plan that was calculated to provide us with a life that was both enjoyable as well as acceptable in every way.

The Charles Lindberg story back in the 1930's was even more prominent across the country than anything that has happened since, except the second world war. It was F. Scott Fitzgerald who said, "Show me a hero, and I will write you a tragedy". In the beginning, Charles Lindberg was a national hero. He later debated with President Roosevelt about the insanity of entering the war against Germany. Prior to that time, he loaded a plane with gas which was almost too heavy to get off the ground in an attempt to cross the Atlantic ocean. Prior to his effort, six men had died trying to do the same thing. Of course we all know that this effort in May 1927, did prove successful, and Lindberg became an instant hero worldwide.

The tragic part of the story came when Lindberg's three year old son was kidnapped. Naturally the kidnapper wanted money. He did pick up $50,000 in marked bills. Unfortunately, one Bruno Hauptman a carpenter, had left a ladder against the house where the boy was taken. In addition, several of the marked bills were later found in Bruno's garage. His trial was probably advertized world wide more than the O.J. Simpson event. It was interesting to see Bruno disagree with the prosecuting attorney, and declare his innocence even when he was executed some 13 months later.

About the Author

Ralph G. Willie, B.S., D.D. S. has been retired from his major profession for years. Along the way, he has engaged in other business activities. These adventures have led to this writing.

It would be helpful if one could always depend upon someone else to manage his money, and reap a profit. This does not seem to happen. Once most people receive your funds, they become theirs, and little else matters. Some of those ventures are portrayed here. Names are eleminated.

All of us are blessed with certain God-given talents. How those talents are exercised is the story of our lives. It seems to be that all of us tend to "reach out," for something more. Reading the *Wall Street Journal* daily is not enough. We need to gain experience, and invest our abilities in such things as real estate licenses, buying and selling, and learning how to manage. Flying an airplane is insufficient.

The recent capture of Saddam Hussein relieved the world of another undesirable dictator. Removal of his activities should prove to be halpful for Iraq and the Arab world. May our country also benefit from an increased appreciation of human value as a result.

Printed in the United States
39341LVS00006B/133-138